back to the
KITCHEN

back to the KITCHEN

FREDDIE PRINZE JR.

with RACHEL WHARTON

75 DELICIOUS, REAL RECIPES (& TRUE STORIES)
from a FOOD-OBSESSED ACTOR

Foreword by
SARAH MICHELLE GELLAR

RODALE.

RODALE
wellness

Live happy. Be healthy. Get inspired.

Sign up today to get exclusive access to our authors, exclusive bonuses,
and the most authoritative, useful, and cutting-edge information on health,
wellness, fitness, and living your life to the fullest.

Visit us online at RodaleWellness.com
Join us at RodaleWellness.com/Join

Rodale books may be purchased for business or promotional use or for special sales.
For information, please write to:
Special Markets Department, Rodale, Inc., 733 Third Avenue, New York, NY 10017

Printed in the United States of America

Rodale Inc. makes every effort to use acid-free ∞, recycled paper ♻.

Book design by Rae Ann Spitzenberger
Photographs by Ellen Silverman
Photo on page 7 is by Shutterstock/Svetoslav Radkov

Library of Congress Cataloging-in-Publication Data is on file with the publisher.

ISBN-13: 978–1–62336–692–6

Distributed to the trade by Macmillan

2   4   6   8   10   9   7   5   3   1   hardcover

Follow us @RodaleBooks on

We inspire and enable people to improve their lives and the world around them.
rodalewellness.com

*To Sarah, Charlotte,
Rocky, and Kathy*

CONTENTS

FOREWORD

Pretty much from the first day I met Freddie, long before he became my husband, I was impressed by his skills in the kitchen. It is so much more than just talent. And even more than creativity. It's love. He is so incredibly passionate about both food and the chemistry involved in creating flavors. I truly believe what makes his food so special is the little bit of him he puts in every meal. He feels genuine reward from the look of enjoyment when people taste his cooking. Before Freddie, I thought cooking was simply making food to eat. Now I understand it's about the experience. The kitchen is where life slows down for a bit, and the simple pleasures take over. It's where true connections are made.

I know I've been entirely spoiled having Freddie in my kitchen for the last 15 years, and not just because my friends constantly remind me. And to be honest, it almost makes me feel a bit guilty. Maybe that's why for the last few years I've been hounding him about writing a cookbook. His skills are way too unique not to share. (Honestly, there are times I pass on going out to dinner, because I know the meal at my house will be better.) I started to feel like the nagging wife: I don't think a meal went by where I didn't say at least once, "This is better than anything I've ever seen in a cookbook."

And then it happened. I started to see Freddie writing things down as he cooked (something he had never done before), and I knew he had begun the journey. I have been all too eager to be a tester for him as he altered his meals. I can honestly tell you I have, more than once, sampled every meal in this book, and now I cannot be happier that he is finally ready to share these delicacies with all of you. Freddie has taught me that cooking is "a practice, not a perfect." Keep that in mind as you read this book. And in case he forgets to tell you, remember his real secret ingredient is love.

SARAH MICHELLE GELLAR

INTRODUCTION

I didn't learn how to throw a football until I was out of high school, so no chance of playing in the Super Bowl for me. Instead, I learned to make veal a dozen different ways. My mom said the kitchen was a better place for my brainy-brain, and plus, she wasn't into sports. What she was into, and very, very good at, was cooking. She could make any dish, from any restaurant, just by tasting it. She was a Jedi in the kitchen, even without attending any kind of culinary institute. She cooked because she loved it, and more important, she made sure that I did, too. I came to understand there's an incredible power in making people a meal—in having them take a bite and it being so good they praise whichever god they believe in.

So instead of throwing spirals and scoring touchdowns, I learned to make Italian sauces and use the New Mexican chiles grown near Albuquerque, where we lived. My mother made everything with fresh ingredients and always prepared meals we could make together as a family. That was just the two of us, and since she worked all day, it meant we were often cooking dinner at 9 or 10 at night—but I loved it: We lived in the desert, so we could sit on the back porch every single night of the year and just chill, together.

My mother encouraged me to explore: If I wanted to try miso soup, we'd make miso soup, or cook any kind of fish I wanted to try. She also showed me how to build flavor with fresh herbs from our garden and find great combinations both by trial and error and by being open to exploration and new ideas. Though her obsession with great food did border on insane at times: I wasn't allowed to date vegetarians, and if I did, I was too smart to bring them home. She would rationalize this rule through science by saying, *Our teeth dictate our diet, and our teeth are meant to eat everything!* (Humans are omnivores, after all.)

I've loved cooking ever since. During my summer trips to Boquerón, Puerto Rico, to visit my paternal grandmother on her little farm, I learned still more.

We would eat fresh eggs and fresh chicken . . . fresh, as in still-clucking-until-recently fresh. However, when she fried it up and I crunched into a piece of that yummy meat, all my issues with watching its death faded away. (My own fried chicken recipe is now the New Mexican–Puerto Rican combo on page 76—plus, you don't have to slaughter your own bird.)

When I graduated from high school and was getting ready to move to California to follow in my father's footsteps and take over the family business (acting!), my mom had encouraged (insisted!) that I attend cooking school as a backup plan. You never go hungry, she said. She was right. But I was all set to go to the Le Cordon Bleu College of Culinary Arts in Pasadena when I got my first real acting gig, and the rest is history. (Our argument over whether I should go actually created that fried chicken, by the way.)

I never stopped loving good food or cooking. After a long day of filming, back when I was still a night owl and a nomad going from gig to gig, I'd go hang out at restaurants in London or in Sydney after work, talking to chefs. I liked what they ate, I liked what they cooked, I liked what they drank, and I made them teach me more about it all. Back home in Los Angeles, I'd do the same thing.

Now with two kids of my own, I cook almost every meal for them, recipes I learned from Mom, recipes I learned along the way at my favorite restaurants around the globe, some recipes I made up on my own. My 5-year-old daughter contributes often to the process, cutting herbs from the garden or standing on a stool, just like I used to when my mother cooked with me. My mother did it, now I do it, and so on down the line with my kids, with luck. She helps me with my mother's tomato soup (it's creamless, and the *best*, and you can find the recipe on page 136), bakes cookies and cakes, and watches cartoons at breakfast while I cook and serve her, the royal princess. Her involvement has made eating a breeze most days . . . most. The younger boy . . . well, he's 3 and just getting old enough to help in the kitchen, but he already eats everything. He'd eat me if he could.

It's important to me that they learn what my mom taught me: to cook with real ingredients, from scratch and with love, and that if you have a full belly at the end of the day, it doesn't matter where you sleep. I wanted to write this cookbook partially for them, but also because I grew tired of hearing my friends and colleagues saying they didn't know how to cook.

That's why every one of these recipes that I will share with you guys is food I make for my family, often. They work. Some are meals for the parents and the kids. Some are meals for when the kids finally go to bed. Most are meals you can make easily and quickly and forget about counting calories, because you'll already be eating right. And some are meals that my wife will admit are the ones she keeps me around for.

If you like Mexican food, get ready for a different kind of heat from New Mexico's rightfully famous chiles, and of course the state's legendary green chile chicken enchiladas. I'll share my easy New Mexico pulled pork, and for breakfast, you'll even get green eggs con jamón. (That's ham, to gringos.) From my Puerto Rican side, you're getting fish my way (lots of citrus)! But also simple pastas, salads and soups, and lots of fresh vegetables that should be your everyday go-tos. I call this cookbook *Back to the Kitchen* because cooking was my first passion: These are all recipes from me, my mother, my friends, and some other special family members whose food I think is just too good to deny anyone.

Enjoy!

FREDDIE PRINZE JR.

EGGS & BREAKFASTS

Chapter 1

THE ROCK'S CINNAMON PANCAKES SERVES 4

These are my little jiu-jitsu master's pancakes—my son's favorite breakfast. I make these cakes—which are taller and heartier than Parker Posey's on page 9—with my kids, and I encourage you to do so, too. I find my daughter, Charlotte, tells me everything going on her in her evil-genius mind, but only while we are cooking. If I ask her how school was after she gets home, I get the standard answer: "good." If we're cooking, unprompted, she'll spill all her secrets: "So, Daddy, yesterday at school we got to meet a real-life iguana!" Me learn quick-like: Me cook more with my kids. My mom also made pancakes like this for me. She would chop fruit up, add it to the pancake syrup, and warm it all in the microwave at the end. You want to add fruit right to your batter instead? Do it. How will I know? The point is, do your own thing!

1 cup all-purpose flour

1 tablespoon sugar

1 teaspoon ground cinnamon

1 teaspoon baking powder

½ teaspoon baking soda

⅛ teaspoon salt

1 cup buttermilk

1 large egg, beaten

3 tablespoons unsalted butter, melted, plus 2 to 4 tablespoons for cooking the pancakes

1 In a large bowl, stir together the flour, sugar, cinnamon, baking powder, baking soda, and salt. Gently whisk in the buttermilk and egg. When the batter is smooth, mix in the melted butter.

2 Heat a large skillet over medium heat. When the skillet is hot, add 2 tablespoons of butter. As soon as it is melted and sizzling, make the pancakes a few at a time. I use ¼ cup of batter per these pancakes, adding more butter if necessary after each batch. Pay attention, as these will cook fast: Flip them when you see bubbles form on the top and the bottom is GBD! (Golden Brown Delicious.) And then, once the other side is GBD, and the top no longer feels loose or jiggly to the touch, remove them from the skillet immediately. For best results, try not to flip them more than once.

3 Keep warm or serve right away, with plain syrup . . . or syrup with chopped, fresh fruit warmed in the microwave, just like Mom.

BISCUITS WITH GREEN CHILE SAUSAGE GRAVY SERVES 6

These are no joke. I made these many years ago while working on a movie in Vancouver with a wonderful actor, Monica Potter, and Adam Shankman, the always awesome director and choreographer.* Neither New Mexico green chiles, pasillas, nor Anaheims—my go-to green chiles—are abundant in Vancouver, so I improvised with equal parts poblanos and jalapeños. They gave my sausage gravy a slightly different flavor, but it was still a solid recipe—and if you can't find the proper green chiles, they'll work for you, too. In fact, both of those two ate my breakfast, and probably both of them wanted to marry me. Hey, don't forget, I was dreamy back then, and single until the wife found out I was on the market. She swiped me up quick-like.

GREEN CHILE SAUSAGE GRAVY
1 tablespoon unsalted butter

1 pound bulk breakfast sausage or sausage patties, crumbled

3 tablespoons chopped fresh New Mexico green chiles or a substitute (see "About New Mexico Chiles," page 7)

2 cups heavy cream

2 tablespoons honey

½ tablespoon freshly ground black pepper

BISCUITS
2 cups all-purpose flour, plus more for dusting

2 teaspoons baking powder

½ teaspoon baking soda

1 teaspoon salt

1½ sticks (6 ounces) very cold unsalted butter, cubed, plus 1 tablespoon melted butter

1 cup milk

Snipped chives and coarse sea salt, for serving (optional)

1 Preheat the oven to 425°F. Lightly grease a baking sheet.

2 Make the gravy: In a medium saucepan, melt the butter over medium-low heat. Add the sausage and the chiles and cook, stirring occasionally, until the chiles have softened and the sausage has started to brown, about 5 minutes.

recipe continues

* and Holy Reverend who eventually married me and my wife!

3 Add the cream and bring the mixture to a boil, then quickly reduce to a low simmer. Add the honey and black pepper and simmer, stirring frequently, until the mixture is thick and gravy-like, 12 to 15 minutes. Taste for salt and black pepper—it should be slightly sweet. Your gravy is done and ridunkulous: Keep it warm until the biscuits are ready.

4 Make the biscuits: In a large bowl, combine 1 cup of the flour with the baking powder, baking soda, and salt. Add the cold butter, using a pastry cutter, a fork, or 2 knives to quickly break it into smaller pieces and blend it with the dry ingredients. Mix in the remaining 1 cup flour.

5 Add the milk and stir gently with a fork or your hands until the biscuit dough just comes together and all the flour is moistened. Not long, as you don't want the butter to melt—the dough should be lumpy and rough.

6 Dust a work surface with flour and scrape the dough out of the bowl with a spatula, then knead it once or twice with your hands until it just comes together. Roll it out into a 1-inch-thick slab, then cut out rounds or squares (2-inch rounds will give you about a dozen, but I like small rounds so that I end up with 14 to 16 biscuits).

7 Lay the biscuits out on the greased baking sheet, glaze their tops with the melted butter, and bake until GBD (Golden Brown Delicious!), 12 to 15 minutes.

8 To serve, I put some gravy down on each plate, reheating it slightly if necessary. I lay one biscuit down on the plate and cover it with gravy. Then I take a second biscuit, tear it open, and stack it open-faced on the plate, one side slightly overlapping the other. Add even more gravy and garnish with chives and sea salt if desired.

SECRET TRICK: If you want to go the instant route for the biscuits, I'm not watching, and even if I was, I don't judge. They're fast and easy, I get it. However, if it's the weekend, and the kids are playing together, and you have a few extra minutes, just go for it. Biscuits are way easier than you think. It's also smart to make the gravy first, because homemade biscuits are best when served piping hot.

ABOUT NEW MEXICO CHILES

Anyone smart who has spent any time in New Mexico, where I grew up, can't live without the state's chiles. Those are the green or Hatch chiles (named for the village of the same name where many are grown), and also New Mexico red chiles, which are green chiles that have been fully ripened and then dried, which imparts an almost buttery taste. These varieties of chiles have varying degrees of heat, but all have a pungent flavor that is unlike any chiles anywhere else, thanks both to genetics and New Mexico's unique climate. They are the backbone of New Mexican cooking. I get pounds of both delivered to my house in California by a friend.

For those not lucky enough to know a local, there are many, many growers with online sites to ship you both kinds. The green ones usually come roasted and frozen but are sometimes shipped fresh during harvest season. Dried red ones usually come tied together into dried chile bouquets known as *ristras*. You can also order green chile powder and the more widely used red chile powder, which is often now available right on the spice rack of many ordinary grocery stores. If you want to make any recipe where I specify New Mexico chiles or chile powder, I recommend you find some from websites like diazfarms.com or newmexicanconnection.com, as it can make all the difference.

But if you must substitute or are in a hurry, for roasted green chiles I usually suggest substituting chiles with some flavor and a little heat, like *pasilla* chiles or Anaheim chiles from California, which are easily found around the country at places like Whole Foods Market. Most grocery stores also carry canned green Hatch-style chiles, which will also work. You could also use an equal mix of poblanos—which have very little heat but a lot of chile flavor—and a hot chile like a jalapeño. For a substitute for the dried red chiles, ancho chiles have a little less heat than the New Mexico chile but still that warm, buttery flavor.

Note that from good sources, New Mexico chiles often come in a range of heat levels, from pretty mild to pretty hot, and you can buy what you prefer. The recipes in this book are based on my preference for chiles with a little bit of heat.

PARKER POSEY'S PANCAKES SERVES 4

Pancakes always make me think of Parker Posey. She is one of my favorite actors, and I was fortunate enough to work with her on one of my very first jobs, The House of Yes. *Parker is amazing. Every choice she makes on camera is courageous and bold. Few have the guts to try what she executes in every film. I loved her just as much in real life. I was just 19 at the time, and she spoke to me about living in hotels all over the place, and her ritual of ordering pancakes and cleaning the sink with Ajax, which she would steal from housekeeping. (Again, robbing the housekeeping trolley, courageous.) She told me the pancakes at the Chateau Marmont hotel in Los Angeles "weren't fit to eat and couldn't be described as breakfast to any living creature on this planet." My goal then was to make her the pancakes my mother made me: The lemon zest always makes 'em feel and taste fresh and light. I arrived very early on the final day of shooting the film and got to work. I burned three by putting too much pressure on myself. Finally I figured out the stupid stove and busted out a dozen in about 20 minutes. Pancake God!!! Unfortunately, at that point I didn't understand what a call sheet was and didn't realize Parker had already wrapped. The scene I thought she was in was being played by her character as a young girl. (That was Rachael Leigh Cook, with a killer performance, by the way! Pre* She's All That.*) When you make these, make an extra for Parker. Ya never know—she's so cool, she just may knock on your door one day.*

2 cups all-purpose flour

3 tablespoons sugar

2½ teaspoons baking powder

½ teaspoon salt

2 large eggs

1½ cups whole or low-fat milk

1½ teaspoons grated lemon zest

2 to 4 tablespoons unsalted butter

recipe continues

1 In a large bowl, stir together the flour, sugar, baking powder, and salt. In a medium bowl, mix together the eggs, milk, and lemon zest. Slowly add the milk mixture to the flour mixture. Stir until the mixture is smooth.

2 Heat a large skillet over medium to medium-high heat. When the skillet is hot, add 2 tablespoons of the butter. As soon as it is melted and sizzling, make the pancakes a few at a time. I use a soup ladle and add 2 pancakes per ladleful. Add more butter to the skillet as necessary as you make the rest of the pancakes.

3 Let the pancakes cook until the tops begin to bubble, 3 to 5 minutes. The edges should be just dry and the bottoms should be beginning to brown. Gently slide a spatula under each pancake and turn it over.

4 Let them cook until the other side begins to brown—another 3 to 5 minutes—and the centers are no longer jiggly to the touch: They're ready to go. Serve them immediately or keep them warm in the oven until all the pancakes are done.

SECRET TRICK: Now, if you're awesome, you'll slice up some bananas or take a handful of blueberries and add them to the cakes about 30 seconds after the pour. Both go great with the lemon zest. You can also try sprinkling these with powdered sugar and squeezing on the juice from the lemon you just zested.

MOM'S GRAND MARNIER FRENCH TOAST
SERVES 4

When I was 8 years old, my mom's friend loaned us their cabin for a weekend during summer break. I got to bring friends and my cousin Chris—my mom was always pretty cool. Her brother—my uncle Jim, an Army veteran, from whom both my son and I get our middle names—taught her a lot, and on that camping trip, she built a big campfire for us. She made us find big rocks to make a circle, then we had to gather wood, and then dig a shallow hole into the ground. (We basically did all the lame stuff, she got to do all the fire fun.) We also got to stay up late, until eventually we crashed out in bunk beds, and when we woke up, we smelled the sweetest smell a man has ever smelled in the morning: bacon and this crazy French toast my mom was making way back in 1984. We went insane. It had orange juice, alcohol, and powdered sugar— the camping breakfast of champions. We loved it. My mom regretted making it, because it was all my cousin Chris and I would ask for after that. It's still a great weekend dish for the family—a once-in-a-while treat. It's very good with bacon and eggs.

4 large eggs

¼ cup Grand Marnier

2 tablespoons freshly squeezed orange juice

¾ cup half-and-half

2 tablespoons granulated sugar

1 tablespoon grated orange zest

½ teaspoon vanilla extract

8 slices soft white bread, sliced ¾ inch thick

4 tablespoons unsalted butter

Powdered sugar and maple syrup, for serving

1 Preheat the oven to 200°F.

2 In a large bowl, whisk together the eggs, Grand Marnier, orange juice, half-and-half, granulated sugar, orange zest, and vanilla.

recipe continues

3 Dip each slice of bread in the egg mixture and layer them in a large baking dish. Pour the remaining liquid over the bread and let it rest for 20 minutes, so the bread can absorb the egg mixture.

4 In your largest skillet, melt 2 tablespoons of the butter over medium-high heat. Add 3 to 4 of the bread slices and cook until GBD (Golden Brown Delicious) on both sides, about 3 minutes per side. When done, place the slices on a baking sheet and keep them in the oven to stay warm.

5 Add the remaining 2 tablespoons of butter to the skillet and repeat the above with the remaining bread.

6 Dust with powdered sugar and drizzle with maple syrup just before serving.

SECRET TRICK: These days instead of plain white bread, I use challah. (Holla!!!!)

HOW TO ROAST CHILES

1   Bring one eye of your gas stovetop to medium-high or preheat your broiler. (Or if you're already grilling, you can just do this outside on the grill.)

2   If using the stovetop, place the chile directly on the eye over the flame (trust me) and blacken it on all sides, using tongs to turn the pepper over so every surface is charred. You aren't burning it, don't worry. If using the broiler, just place the pepper under the flame and roast, turning with tongs until all sides are blackened and charred.

3   Remove the pepper from the heat and place it in a small resealable plastic bag for 2 to 3 minutes. This will steam the skin and make it very easy to remove.

4   Take the roasted pepper out of the bag and place it on a cutting board. Holding the pepper in place by the stem with one hand, rake a regular dinner fork gently down the sides of the pepper, lightly piercing the skin with the tines, then using them to pull the skin off gently. It should peel right off with little effort. There might be a few little black flecks of char left on the chile. That's okay. You can also remove the seeds from the chile with a spoon if you are wary of too much heat (or are roasting multiple chiles). Just be sure to wear plastic gloves when handling the seeds and membrane and to wash your cutting board well after you prep the chiles. At this point, you can store the chile in the refrigerator for up to a week.

THE GREEN SAUCE MAKES ABOUT 1 CUP

The Green Sauce, or chile verde *sauce, is a staple in our kitchen. It goes with everything, is full of flavor, and is easy to make with only three main ingredients. You can easily double or even triple the recipe: A good rule of thumb is one chile to one avocado to one clove of garlic. This works great as a side sauce for breakfast, with the steak recipe on page 28, for the nachos on page 63, or you can use it as your sauce for any kind of taco, like the ones on page 44. Or instead of regular guacamole as a dip: My daughter lives to dip. Chips, chicken, bread, pasta, scrambled eggs on toast—anything that can be dipped, you better believe is going in. She's pretty much the LeBron James of food dunking. My son is still on amateur status as far as his food dipping and dunking skills go. Currently, he has more of a mash-and-spread style.**

1 large green New Mexico green chile or a substitute (see "About New Mexico Chiles," page 7), roasted (see opposite page)

1 avocado

1 clove garlic

¼ to ½ teaspoon salt

⅛ to ¼ teaspoon freshly ground black pepper

2 to 4 tablespoons extra virgin olive oil

1 In a food processor, combine the roasted chile, avocado flesh, garlic, ¼ teaspoon salt, ⅛ teaspoon black pepper, and 2 tablespoons of the oil and give it a buzz till the texture of the sauce is smooth and creamy.

2 Drizzle in more oil as necessary and taste for salt and pepper. This will keep for about 2 days in the fridge.

SECRET TRICK: I use roasted green chiles all the time, so when I make them, I usually roast a bunch, store them well covered in the fridge, and use them for different things throughout the next week or so.

*So unlike Kurtis Blow, basketball will not be his favorite sport. He will not watch them run up and down the court. (Yes, I do know old-school rap better than you. Just Google the 1984 song "Basketball" if you don't know what I'm talking about.)

SECRET TRICK: In the book, how did Sam I Am actually get that cranky old man to eat his breakfast? He put it in a burrito, of course. Anytime I can't get my kids to try something, I wrap a tortilla around it: I'll scramble eggs with leftover chopped cooked zucchini or broccoli—which you could even add here—then throw a soft flour tortilla down on a plate and fold them up. They can go low-carb in their thirties. I don't sweat that kind of stuff with my kids.

GREEN (CHILE) EGGS AND HAM SERVES 2

Like most kids, one of the first stories my kids ever heard was Green Eggs and Ham *by the good Dr. Seuss. (Or* Juevos Verdes con Jamón, *since we have the book both in Spanish and in English.) My daughter didn't believe me the first time I told her I was going to make green eggs and ham. Charlotte went bananas for this breakfast, and she went and told her mother, who came downstairs, saw GREEN eggs, and smiled ear to ear. (This is a precoffee smile, people! Think about how rarely you grin before that first cup—'nuff said!) You can also use the pesto on page 157 instead of my standard* chile verde *sauce.*

4 slices bacon

4 large eggs

¼ cup the Green Sauce (page 15), plus more for garnish

4 medium flour tortillas (8 inch diameter), warmed

1 Line a plate with paper towels and heat a large nonstick skillet over medium-high heat. Cook the bacon in the skillet until it is browned and crispy, about 10 minutes.

2 While the bacon cooks, beat the eggs together in a medium bowl until blended, then gently stir in the green sauce until it is well incorporated.

3 When the bacon is cooked, let it drain on the paper towels and remove all but a tablespoon or two of bacon grease from the skillet.

4 Bring the reserved bacon grease back up to medium-low heat, then add the egg mixture. Cook, scraping the eggs up from the bottom and sides from time to time with a wooden spoon or spatula, until the eggs are fluffy and cooked through.

5 Serve with the bacon, warm tortillas, and more green sauce.

MY MORNING OMELET

SERVES 1 VERY HUNGRY FREDDIE OR 2 REGULAR ADULTS

This is my main breakfast, and how I start most mornings. I eat this before I train or roll jiu jitsu. I'll also do some instant plain oatmeal with honey and blueberries on the side. I usually don't have a lot of time, so I do all the dicing the night before and toss the veggies precut into the fridge. After that, it all comes together in minutes.

4 large eggs

¼ cup diced onion

¼ cup diced green bell pepper

2 ounces diced ham (about ½ cup)

1 loosely packed cup fresh spinach, slivered

1 tablespoon olive oil

2 ounces shredded Monterey Jack cheese (about ¾ cup)

1 Crack the eggs into a small bowl and beat them well with a fork or whisk, then set them aside.

2 In another small bowl, combine the onion, bell pepper, ham, and spinach.

3 In a nonstick medium skillet, heat the oil over medium heat. Add the veggies and ham. Cook until the onion begins to turn translucent and most of the liquid from the spinach and pepper is gone, 5 to 6 minutes.

4 Pour in the egg mixture, swirling to let it coat the pan, and cook until the eggs just begin to set, 2 to 3 minutes.

5 Sprinkle the cheese evenly over the top, and when the sides of the omelet are firm enough to handle, about 5 more minutes, use a flexible nonstick spatula to fold half of the omelet over the other.

6 Cook until the eggs are set in the middle—another minute or two—and slide the omelet right out of the pan onto your plate.

THE DINER SPECIAL (AKA BACON & EGGS OVER EASY, WITH WHOLE WHEAT TOAST)

My girl had eggs over easy at a New York City diner when she was 3 years old, and for more than a year it was the only way she would have her eggs and bacon. Luckily a little bit of runny yolk is really simple to do if you follow one major rule: Low and Slow. (If you have a cast iron skillet, you know this works best in that. If not, nonstick is fine, too.)

Let the pan get hot for 2 to 3 minutes—between medium-low and low is the way to go—then I give the pan a quick spray of cooking spray and start with 2 slices of bacon. Low heat, then flip the bacon after 2 minutes, two times. Set the bacon aside on a paper towel and pour out the grease. Give the pan a quick wipe with a paper towel and return it to the stovetop. Another quick blast of cooking spray, and add 2 small or medium eggs, cracking them right into the pan. As soon as the edges firm up, take your spatula and gently flip the eggs over. Just 1 minute on the second side—watch the clock—and then you are ready to eat.

I serve this to my daughter with 2 slices of whole wheat toast on the side, but these days Charlie makes it into a breakfast sandwich and lets the yolk run everywhere. (And she wonders why my wife and I make her wear a bib over her school clothes at breakfast.) Of course, you can multiply this recipe for however many diner customers you want to serve.

PROTEIN POWER SERVES 1

An easy workout drink, which comes with Dr. Freddie P's scientific tip of the day: Don't have your shake until AFTER your workout. When you finish a strong workout, your body will crush nearly anything you put in it. It wants to use whatever you eat/drink for you. If you go with healthy proteins, vitamins, and minerals, you'll get the benefits actors and athletes get from their trainers feeding them the same info. (I like whey-based protein powder, by the way.)

10 ounces fat-free milk or milk substitute

1 scoop protein powder
3 tablespoons honey

12 blueberries

Place the milk, protein powder, honey, and blueberries in a blender. Pulse for about 20 seconds.

MEAT

TRICOLOR SALAD WITH SAUTÉED SHALLOT DRESSING AND FLANK STEAK

SERVES 4

The best salads have plenty of colors and flavors and a lot of crunch, like this one. I make it when the weather is warmer and I have the grill going all the time, but you could cook the steak on the stovetop. I sometimes add a sliced avocado, and you could also toss on a few toasted nuts, pumpkin seeds, or crumbles of cheese. Or you could sub in any grilled protein you want: chicken, pork, tofu; or skip it and serve this as a fancy side salad.

SHALLOT DRESSING

4 tablespoons extra virgin olive oil

2 shallots, diced

1 tablespoon balsamic vinegar

Salt and freshly ground black pepper

STEAK

1½ pounds flank steak

1 teaspoon salt

1 teaspoon freshly ground black pepper

SALAD

1 head romaine lettuce, washed, dried, and roughly torn

1 small head radicchio, washed, dried, and roughly torn

1 Belgian endive, thinly sliced

1 pint (10 to 12 ounces) cherry tomatoes, halved if desired

1 shallot, thinly sliced

1 Persian (mini) cucumber, thinly sliced

1 Make the dressing first: In a small skillet, heat 1 tablespoon of the oil over medium-low heat. Add the shallots and cook until they are clear and soft, about 5 minutes. Remove them from the pan and let them cool completely.

2 When the shallots are cool, transfer them to a small bowl or a jar with a lid and add the remaining 3 tablespoons oil, the vinegar, and a pinch each of salt and pepper. Whisk or shake to combine. Taste for salt, pepper, and vinegar, adding more to taste. Set aside while you grill the steak.

recipe continues

3 Prepare a grill or heat a grill pan or large skillet to medium-high. Season the flank steak with the salt and pepper. Grill the steak until it is cooked through to your liking, about 5 minutes per side for medium-rare (a thermometer inserted into the center will registers 145°F) or 8 minutes per side for medium (a thermometer will register 160°F). Remove from the heat and let rest for at least 5 minutes.

4 Slice the steak against the grain (meaning perpendicular to the grain) into $^3/_4$-inch-thick strips, and then again into 1-inch pieces. Set aside while you make the salad.

5 Assemble the salad: In a large salad or serving bowl, combine the romaine, radicchio, and endive and toss well with a tablespoon or two of the shallot dressing, enough to fully coat the lettuces. Add the cherry tomatoes, sliced shallot, cucumber, and steak and gently toss again. Add more dressing as needed, gently tossing to combine, and taste for salt, pepper, and vinegar, adding more to taste.

(EASY AS PIE) MARINATED SKIRT STEAK WITH CHERRY TOMATO AND AVOCADO SALSA

SERVES 4

First steak I ever learned to make. And like they say in Gracie jiu-jitsu, which I have studied for decades, "The first things you learn are the last things you'll forget." This steak is awesome: easy and simple to both prepare and to grill. If I have time, I'll roast a few beets early on, fridge them, cut them into cubes, and toss those in the salsa as well. You aren't getting a healthier steak than this. Don't skip the step of patting the skirt steak dry: We do this to make sure we grill the meat and not steam it—which with too much liquid on there would happen.

2 pounds skirt steak

1 cup orange juice

1 cup reduced-sodium soy sauce

1 pint (10 to 12 ounces) large cherry tomatoes, halved

1 avocado, cubed

1 tablespoon fresh lime juice

2 teaspoons olive oil

Salt and freshly ground black pepper

1 Clean any extra membrane and fat from the steak. Place the steak in a large zip-seal bag and add the orange juice and soy sauce. Press the air out of the bag and seal it, and let it marinate in the refrigerator for at least 1 hour 30 minutes; 3 to 8 hours is even better.

2 Meanwhile, in a small bowl, toss the tomatoes with the avocado, lime juice, and olive oil. Season with a pinch each of salt and pepper and add more of either or more lime juice as needed. Refrigerate the salsa until you are ready to serve the steak.

3 When it is time to make the steak, prepare a grill to high or grease a medium skillet with a small film of oil and heat over high heat.

4 Remove the steak from the marinade and pat both sides very dry with some paper towels. Grill or pan-fry the steak until it is cooked through to your liking—about 5 minutes per side for medium-rare (until a thermometer inserted into the center registers 145°F) or about 8 minutes per side for medium (a thermometer will register 160°F).

5 Remove the steak from the heat and let it rest for at least 5 minutes before slicing it into $1/2$-inch-thick strips against the grain of the meat (meaning perpendicular to the grain), which helps make the meat more tender.

6 Serve the steak topped with the cold cherry tomato and avocado salsa.

HONEY-CAYENNE GRILLED CHOPS

SERVES 2

The honey and the chile powder in these chops—by which I mean either the magical pig or equally delicious lamb—are going to stand out, but in the end, the sweet takes over rather than the spicy. And if you use ancho chile powder instead of the New Mexico red, you can tame the heat a bit more. Ancho has less heat than the New Mexico, but still that warm, buttery flavor. When I combine that with honey drizzled on top, then grill or sear in a hot skillet, it's game on. Better still, this is a simple summer dinner, because it both tastes best and is easiest cooked out-of-doors. You want to grill this on a medium to medium-high heat to prevent flame-ups, which may affect the taste of the meat. (And just remember to always clean your grill before you use it!) When I grill this dish, I serve it with baby broc and baked potatoes, each wrapped tightly in heavy-duty foil and tossed right on the grill. It takes about 50 minutes for the potatoes, and 15 to 20 for the green vegetables, so I put them on first. You can also make this dish in a skillet, in which case you'll want to cook the vegetables in the oven.

¼ teaspoon salt

¼ teaspoon freshly ground black pepper

1 teaspoon garlic powder

1 teaspoon onion powder

1 teaspoon ancho chile powder or New Mexico red chile powder

1 teaspoon cayenne pepper

Cooking spray or 2 tablespoons olive oil (see "About Cooking Spray," page 32)

2 bone-in pork chops (1½ inches thick) or 4 double-boned lamb chops

2 tablespoons honey

1 In a small bowl, mix together the salt, black pepper, garlic powder, onion powder, chile powder, and cayenne pepper.

2 Spray the pork chops on both sides with cooking spray, or brush them with 1 tablespoon of the oil and season both sides with the spice mixture. Drizzle the honey evenly over both sides of the chops.

recipe continues

3 To grill the chops: Prepare a grill to medium-high. Grill the chops for 5 to 7 minutes per side, or until a thermometer inserted into the center registers 145°F and the juices run clear. Let the chops rest for 5 minutes before serving.

4 To cook the chops on the stovetop: In a medium skillet, heat 1 tablespoon of olive oil over medium heat. Sear the chops on one side—5 to 7 minutes—then flip and cook another 5 to 7 minutes until cooked through, following the temperature guideline above. Let the chops rest for 5 minutes before serving.

SECRET TRICK: I often make this with double-boned lamb chops (which my kids like just as much as pork) or boneless, butterflied pork chops (which end up thinner, which means they will cook even faster than bone-in chops).

About Cooking Spray

I am a fan of spray oils, particularly coconut, which is a healthy fat I use in every form. It adds a subtle, slightly tropical flavor that I use in many things I cook. Spray oils let you coat ingredients with oil without using too much of it, which is especially handy when you are grilling things. If you prefer not to use sprays, brush the food to be grilled with olive oil. Just use a light hand, so the food doesn't flare up as you grill.

LET THE CHOP BE A CHOP

Lamb chops aren't from my mama or from a chef Down Under, even though I spent lots of time there. Instead they are a version of a dish I made for my roommates when I lived in LA in the late '90s. I love lamb for its big flavor. These guys were fast food burger type–guys, and two of them hated lamb, or so they thought. Within a year I had all of them eating right and cooking insanely good food. (By the time I moved out, they would make this dish for me.) I'll admit lamb can taste funny if it isn't done right, and I always say *acquired taste* means "get used to this sucking." So I try and make things taste good the first time . . . so it's only fear my friends have to get over, not bad-tasting food.

Case in point, after I made this for my kids, my daughter, Charlotte, told a friend she loved lamb. Her friend asked her mom to make her lamb, and so she broiled a lamb chop with hardly any seasoning . . . tough meal for a 5-year-old. Charlie's friend hated it and thought my daughter played a mean trick on her. So we had the girl over, and I made dinner and told her we were eating "chops." The little girl had four . . . and these are double-boned. Her mom tripped out. Got excited. Told her kiddo how proud she was she ate lamb . . . tick tick tick . . . boom: "I HATE LAMB!!!! WAAAAAAHHHH!" Oh boy.

Trust me parents. LIE to your kids. Lie, I say! My mom told me everything was chicken, and I now love everything. You let them believe in the Tooth Fairy, or Santa, or crappy old Chanukah Harry. Let them believe the lie of the "chop." By the way, it's a year later and that same kid is now eating oxtail soup and sushi with her folks. What?? In your face!

HOLY $#!% PULLED PORK SERVES 4

This dish actually made my wife curse in front of our daughter. (Charlotte was just a year old and fortunately survived the experience.) I served the pork in small, thick tortillas with some Jack cheese—that's all you really need. Sarah took a big bite and, midchew, let out a "Holy $#!%." For the past few years, I've been messing around with the recipe, just to mix things up, but this is one of our favorite versions. If you can't easily find the New Mexico red chile powder, ancho chile powder is a great-tasting substitute in this dish, but it will be a bit milder. (Go for the New Mexico red whenever you get the chance.) You can simply serve this as I did with shredded cheese and flour tortillas, as they would in my home state of New Mexico, which is a flour tortilla place, or "deconstructed," the way my father's family would have eaten it in Puerto Rico. That way, the pork is served in a bowl with your extras—Spanish rice, whatever green veg is fresh, plus the easy black beans (from the chicken thighs on page 82) and cold sliced cucumbers laid out around it. (What?!?! Try them.) I still add the tortillas on the side so the kids can build their own tacos: It's a fun way to get them to eat well. This is also good with the Green Sauce (page 15).

2 tablespoons olive oil

1 to 1½ pounds pork tenderloin

¼ teaspoon salt

¼ teaspoon freshly ground black pepper

4 cups (32 ounces) chicken stock

2 teaspoons garlic powder

1 heaping tablespoon New Mexico red chile powder or a substitute (see "About New Mexico Chiles," page 7)

1 In a Dutch oven, heat the oil over medium heat. Season the tenderloin with the salt and pepper and then brown both sides, 3 to 5 minutes per side.

2 Add the chicken stock—it won't fully cover the pork—then the spices and bring to a low boil. As soon as you see bubbles, reduce the heat to a simmer, cover the pot, and then walk away for 1 hour 30 minutes. The pork should be fork-tender.

3 Turn off the heat and remove the tenderloin to a cutting board.

4 While the pork rests, bring the liquid remaining in the pot back up to a simmer and let it cook until it is reduced by half, 15 to 20 minutes. Taste for salt.

5 Meanwhile, use a fork to "pull" or shred the pork. (It should just fall apart.) Once the whole tenderloin has been shredded, add it back into the liquid and turn off the heat.

6 Let it sit for 5 minutes before serving, with warm tortillas and shredded cheese or rice and beans.

Family Style

The goal of this dish is really to make dinner as simple as possible, with few ingredients and serious walk-away ability. Instead of hanging around the stove, I mean, I can hang with my family, play Candy Land, or tap out when my daughter proceeds to apply the Gracie jiu-jitsu armlock on me. (She's 5, and just as deadly as any wrestler I met when I worked with WWF as a writer and a cohost.) When the pork is done, I remove it from the liquid and let it rest on a cutting board for about 10 minutes. After that, I give Charlotte a fork and she "pulls" like a pro; it is a true kid-friendly dish what with the cheese-shredding, tortilla-warming, and the most important job . . . tasting. The bottom line is we make this dish as a family. My daughter, if she was allowed to use the stove, could make this by herself at this point. We cook together, play together, and eat together. The cleaning part is somehow on me, though—the help seems to vanish when it comes time to do the dishes. I cook and clean. Brutal, right? Wrong! It's also a win for me (guys, I am speaking to you), because my wife gives me no grief when I want to watch the Golden State Warriors drop 120 points or play Xbox. Your significant others will tell their friends, and their friends will scream in anger that their special someone does NONE of this. . . . Now you are better than all of them, and all you did was 10 minutes of dishes. You're welcome.

PORK ENCHILADAS WITH SHREDDED PORK SAUCE (AKA FRIENDLY *ADOVADA*)

SERVES 4

My mother taught me this dish: The sauce is insane. Insane! It is a riff on a classic New Mexican dish called adovada, *or chile-braised pork. When my mom makes it, she makes individual enchiladas: She lays out 6 flour tortillas, places the shredded meat in each one, then rolls them up and lays them side by side. She then pours the leftover liquid in the pan—now a chile sauce with remnants of the pork—ladle by ladle over the enchiladas. She finishes the dish with a healthy layer of cheese. My recipe is a little faster and turns out more like a casserole, but it is just as delicious. In fact, you might want to make two trays at a time, just to have leftovers.*

3 tablespoons olive oil

1 to 1½ pounds pork tenderloin

1 teaspoon salt

1 teaspoon freshly ground black pepper

7 teaspoons ancho chile powder

4 cups (32 ounces) chicken stock

1 clove garlic, smashed

2 tablespoons unsalted butter

1 bay leaf

6 medium flour tortillas (8 inch diameter)

12 ounces shredded mild cheddar or Monterey Jack cheese, or a blend of the two

1 In a Dutch oven, heat 2 tablespoons of the oil over medium to medium-high heat.

2 Sprinkle the pork evenly on all sides with the salt, pepper, and 2 ½ teaspoons of the chile powder.

3 Brown the tenderloin on both sides in the hot oil, about 7 minutes per side.

4 Slowly add the chicken stock—it will splatter when it hits the hot pot. It will cover anywhere from halfway to just about covering the pork.

recipe continues

5 Add the crushed garlic clove, the remaining 4½ teaspoons chile powder, the butter, and the bay leaf and bring the mixture just to a boil. Reduce the heat, partially cover, and simmer over very low heat until the pork is fork-tender, about 1 hour 30 minutes.

6 Turn off the heat, remove the pork from the liquid, and let it rest for 10 minutes on a cutting board. Meanwhile, taste the cooking liquid for salt.

7 Preheat the oven to 350°F. Grease a 9 x 13-inch baking dish with the remaining 1 tablespoon oil.

8 When the pork has cooled slightly, use your hands or 2 forks to pull the pork into shreds, and if necessary, cut the shreds into more bite-size pieces using a knife or kitchen shears. Return the shredded pork to the liquid and set aside.

9 To prepare the enchiladas my way, lay 2 of the tortillas down flat (they will overlap) in the baking dish. Using a slotted spoon so you scoop up more pork than sauce, spread half of the pork on top of the tortillas, and then sprinkle on one-third of the cheese. Lay down 2 more tortillas and again top them with half of the pork and one-third of the cheese. Lay down the last 2 tortillas and top them with the remaining cheese and pour on whatever sauce remains, using a spatula to scrape out every last drop.

10 Cover with foil and bake for 20 minutes. Remove the foil for the last 5 minutes if you want some crunch to your cheese.

RED FAJITAS SERVES 4

Most fajita recipes call for an overnight marinade. If you have my red chile sauce hanging around, you can make these for dinner even when you're in a hurry. Cooking the vegetables separately from the steak is what keeps their color and flavor bright and strong.

4 tablespoons olive oil

1 red bell pepper, sliced lengthwise into thin strips

1 yellow bell pepper, sliced lengthwise into thin strips

2 medium shallots, thinly sliced

Salt and freshly ground black pepper

1½ pounds skirt or hanger steak, sliced against the grain into ½-inch- to ¼-inch-thick strips

¼ cup Red Chile Sauce (page 65)

8 medium flour tortillas (8 inch diameter), warmed

1 In a medium skillet, heat 2 tablespoons of the oil over medium heat. Add the bell peppers and shallots and a pinch of salt, and cook the vegetables just until they soften but their colors are still bright and strong, 5 to 7 minutes.

2 Turn off the heat, taste for salt, and add a pinch of black pepper. Keep the skillet warm while you cook the steak.

3 Season the steak slices with a generous pinch of salt and black pepper. In a large skillet, heat the remaining 2 tablespoons oil over medium-high heat. When the skillet is hot, add the steak and sear it just until it begins to brown on 1 side, about 4 minutes. Add the red sauce to the meat and stir it in. Cook the meat until it is cooked through, 2 to 3 minutes longer, but keep a close eye, as it cooks quickly.

4 As soon as the steak is cooked through, use tongs or a fork to add just the meat to the veggie pan. Gently toss your ingredients and heat them together over low to medium-low heat for a minute or two.

5 Serve with warm tortillas and any red chile sauce leftover in the pan from cooking the steak.

SECRET TRICK: If you want to be a kitchen ninja, cook the vegetables and the meat at the same time. Start the vegetables right after you add the red sauce, and then add the steak to the veggie pan after 5 minutes.

KIELBASA, SWEET ONION, AND PINEAPPLE SANDWICHES MAKES 6 SANDWICHES

Smoky, juicy kielbasa is a secret weapon. It's already cooked, so all you have to do is heat it through. I dress it up on a sandwich with pineapple, tomato, soft slices of cooked sweet onion, and a little bit of salad. If you can't find onion rolls, go for the soft but sturdy bread that will support the layers of the sandwich but not tear your mouth open as you chomp away. If you like, feel free to dress the buns with your favorite grainy mustard or mayo, or a bit of both.

4 tablespoons extra virgin olive oil

1 tablespoon balsamic vinegar

Salt and freshly ground black pepper

6 slices sweet onion

1 pound smoked kielbasa

6 hearty lettuce leaves

6 onion rolls, warmed

6 slices fresh pineapple

6 large slices tomato

1 Prepare a grill to medium-high or preheat the broiler.

2 In a small bowl or jar with a lid, whisk or shake together 3 tablespoons of the oil, the vinegar, and a pinch each of salt and pepper. Set the vinaigrette aside.

3 Toss the onion slices with the remaining 1 tablespoon of oil and wrap them tightly in 2 layers of foil.

4 Place the foil packet and the sausage on the grill or under the broiler. Cook both until the sausage is browned on both sides, sizzling, and heated through, 5 to 8 minutes per side.

5 Remove both from the grill and let them rest for 5 to 10 minutes.

6 Roughly tear the lettuce into bite-size pieces into a small bowl and dress it with the vinaigrette, tossing to coat. Set aside.

7 Being careful of escaping steam, open the onion packets and season very lightly with salt and pepper.

8 To make the sandwiches, cut the kielbasa into 6 lengths, then butterfly the pieces by slicing them lengthwise almost all the way through. On the bottom of each roll, layer the sausage, a slice of pineapple, a slice of onion, a slice of tomato, and a pile of the dressed lettuce. Drizzle over any leftover dressing or onion juices and top with the other half of the roll. Cut the sandwiches in half and enjoy.

NEW MEX CARNE ASADA TACOS WITH SLICED CUCUMBERS

MAKES 8 TACOS

I've been eating this taco since I was in the first grade at Manzano Day School in Albuquerque, New Mexico. My mother cooked up the carne asada—that's grilled steak—and packed the tacos for my lunch. Sometimes she'd even sprinkle a little Parmesan on the outside. Even cold, these tacos were the highest form of currency from the first through the fifth grade. Kids had never had crunchy cucumbers in a taco, and for one of these tacos I could get anything from your favorite marble to your best G.I. Joe (which was Snake Eyes, for the record). As an adult, I know these are also incredibly simple, healthy, and can save you tons of time. TIME!!!! The second most valuable commodity, behind tacos, of course. Serve this with easy black beans (from the chicken thighs on page 82) and Spanish rice and top with your favorite salsa, my Green Sauce (page 15), or my Red Chile Sauce (page 65). You can make these with corn tortillas if you like, but they'll need to be eaten right away.

1 teaspoon salt

1 teaspoon freshly ground black pepper

1 teaspoon garlic powder

1 teaspoon onion powder

1 tablespoon New Mexico red or ancho chile powder

1 pound skirt steak

Cooking spray, preferably coconut oil

8 small flour tortillas (6 inch diameter), lightly grilled

2 tablespoons fresh lime juice

1 small cucumber, thinly sliced

2 cups shredded Monterey Jack cheese

1 In a small bowl, mix together the salt, pepper, garlic powder, onion powder, and chile powder.

2 Coat the steak with cooking spray, then dust on all sides with the spice blend. Set aside.

recipe continues

3 Prepare a grill or heat a grill pan to medium-high. Grill the steak until it's well charred on the outside, but hopefully just a little pink in the center, 3 to 5 minutes on each side, or until a thermometer inserted into the center registers 145°F for medium-rare. (But this isn't ribeye, so medium-rare isn't a must. Cut yourself some slack.)

4 Remove the meat to a cutting board and let it rest 5 to 10 minutes, then cut it against the grain of the meat (meaning perpendicular to the grain; this helps make the meat more tender) into $1/2$-inch-thick strips and then into $1/2$-inch pieces.

5 Place an equal portion of steak in each tortilla, sprinkle the lime juice over the steak, and top with some sliced cucumber and a generous handful of cheese. Serve hot.

SECRET TRICK: You can marinate the cucumber slices in lime juice to give your tacos a bit of sour zing. If that's your thing, be sure to soak them for at least an hour.

Steak Tacos and the Art of Jiu Jitsu

Chris Sandoval was my best friend in grade school, and I would usually wrestle him for the last carne asada taco. Only-child syndrome and jiu jitsu were my greatest weapons, and so I always won the extra taco, even though he would also purposely eat slower than I would, so he would have more deliciousness to eat when I was already finished. I started to learn the art of fighting from my godfather, Bob Wall, who trained Bruce Lee. He lived in LA, and that's where my mom would send me to learn about my old man and how to protect myself from anyone who might try to throw a punch. (I also learned how to make his excellent hamburger, which you'll find on the opposite page.) P.S. Today my son will fistfight anyone on this planet for steak tacos. He smells the carne asada grilling and starts screaming like a baby tiger.

BURGERS TWO WAYS

The Bob Wall Burger SERVES 4

Every son remembers his first burger with his pops. My godfather, Bob—a professional martial arts master who was a father figure and a huge role model to me after my own father died when I was young—had a full-time housekeeper who cooked as well. (Kicking ass isn't the only thing he's successful at.) She would make him this one burger the same way, every week. She would always leave it in the oven, and he would eat it when he got home from work. I remember so clearly to this day going home with him, when I was staying with him one summer, and him opening the oven: Inside were two delicious-looking burgers, one for each of us. "How does he automatically have burgers?" I thought. The Jetsons were big then, and my 6- or 7-year-old mind was running wild. Years later, I asked for the recipe for those burgers we shared, and it turned out it was my godmother Shana Wall's own recipe. Here it is to share.

1 pound ground beef, at least 15% fat

½ teaspoon garlic powder

½ teaspoon onion powder

½ teaspoon salt

¼ teaspoon freshly ground black pepper

¼ teaspoon cayenne pepper

2 tablespoons soy sauce

1 tablespoon Worcestershire sauce

4 sesame seed buns, warmed

4 leaves butter lettuce

4 slices tomato

Condiments of choice

1 In a large bowl, use your hands to mix the ground beef with the spices, soy sauce, and Worcestershire sauce, and then form the meat into 4 equal patties. Set them aside.

2 Heat a large skillet—large enough to comfortably hold 4 patties without crowding them—over medium-low heat. Cook the burgers, flipping them once, until they reach your desired degree of doneness (about 7 minutes per side for

recipe continues

medium, or until a thermometer inserted into the center registers 160°F and the meat is no longer pink). Let them rest on a cutting board for 5 to 10 minutes before serving.

3 Place the patties on the warmed buns with a lettuce leaf, a slice of tomato, and condiments of your choosing.

The Green Chile Cheeseburger   SERVES 4

This is my favorite burger, period. I've eaten at great burger joints all over the country, and no matter how good it is, I always wish it was this one. Everyone in New Mexico makes these, and just about all of us make it the same way . . . except I like to make mine a double, cause I'm awesome like that. My daughter isn't nuts about ground beef, and I'm not a fan of ground turkey, so for her—and whoever else doesn't want beef—I make the Green Chile Chicken Cheeseburger!!! (Exclamation points make chicken burgers more exciting.) Note that if I could cook everything on the grill, I would. I dig being outside, grillin' in the backyard with our kids and our dog. The dog guards the grill, but it is the only thing she has ever guarded. Ever. If that doesn't convince you to grill these, or you don't have a place to grill, you can use a hot skillet pan or grill pan, or even the broiler.

4 New Mexico green chiles or a substitute, roasted (see steps 1–4, page 14)

Salt and freshly ground black pepper

1 pound ground beef, at least 15% fat

1 teaspoon garlic powder

1 teaspoon onion powder

1 teaspoon cayenne pepper

1 teaspoon ancho chile powder

1 teaspoon Worcestershire sauce

8 thin slices Monterey Jack cheese

4 romaine lettuce leaves

4 brioche buns, warmed

4 slices tomato

1 Dice the chiles and season them with a pinch of salt and black pepper.

2 In a large bowl, use your hands to mix the beef with the garlic powder, onion powder, cayenne, chile powder, $\frac{1}{2}$ teaspoon salt, $\frac{1}{4}$ teaspoon black pepper, and the Worcestershire sauce.

recipe continues

3 To form the patties, cut 2 large sheets of wax paper. Divide the meat mixture into 4 portions and roll them into big meatballs with your hands. Place them on a sheet of wax paper and top with the other sheet. Flatten them with a dinner plate. Trust me: They won't be too thin, as they rise a bit when cooked.

4 Prepare a grill to medium-high; heat a grill pan or skillet to medium-high; or preheat the broiler. Grill, pan-fry, or broil these burgers for about 7 minutes on one side. Flip them, adding one-fourth of the chiles and 2 slices of cheese to the patty so they melt together as the burger continues to cook. Cook the burgers another 5 to 7 minutes for medium, or until a thermometer inserted into the center registers 160°F and the meat is no longer pink. Let the burgers rest for 5 to 10 minutes on a cutting board before you serve them.

5 Place the lettuce on the bottom half of the bun, then the cheese-topped patty, the tomato, and the top half of the bun. Enjoy, it's beastly.

SECRET TRICK: You could also use the cook-it-twice method for the chiles: Dice them and wrap them in foil with a touch of olive oil and cook them at the same time you put the burgers on. When you flip your burgers, place the chile on your burger then pour on the spicy juice and infused olive oil, THEN add your cheese, shredded or not.

MY GODFATHER

When I started elementary school, I had a hard time fitting in. I was quiet and nice (that's changed), and that makes you an easy target. Once my mom picked me up from school and I had a black eye. I was pretty upset, and my widowed mother was heartbroken. She told me I was going to California to meet my godfather, the Great Bob Wall. For those of you who don't know the mixed martial arts game, this man helped invent it. When Bruce Lee moved to America, he trained with Bob Wall. He even put Bob in his movies, because my godfather knew how to make Bruce look even more incredible.

That year my godfather dragged me all over the San Fernando Valley. The father of two great daughters, he proudly introduced to me to living legends like Gene LeBell and Chuck Norris as "my boy, Freddie Jr." These men, and others like Pat Burleson and Jean Jacques Machado, made sure the next fifth-grader (he will remain nameless) who decided to pick on a second-grader (yours truly) was going to get choked out in front of the whole school. I was 6, he was 11, and you do not live that down, ever. And no, I won't let him.

The next summer I got to go see my godfather again. I was by then training in two forms of martial arts in Albuquerque, but all I could think of was training with Bob again. One night we sat and talked and ate a couple of these burgers at a table that overlooked their front yard. He told me my mom had called him and said I whipped a fifth-grader's ass pretty good. "I only leg kicked him," I told Bob, and "then when he fell I took his back and choked him for 6 seconds." Bob starting laughing and asked me if I actually counted to six out loud. When I nodded, he gave me the strongest pat on the head you've ever felt. He told me about my own father, whom he knew well, and then he said, "Now go to bed. Tomorrow I'll teach you the 1-inch punch."

VEAL PICCATA SERVES 4

My mom made this dish when I was growing up, and I didn't think anybody anywhere could make it better . . . until about 15 years ago, when I found an amazing version in London, of all places. (Don't be dense and think the Brits can't cook—that myth died in the '90s. Young men and women inspired by the world's great chefs have completely redefined British cuisine.) Like my mom's version, I don't use flour. Don't freak out, I'm saving you time, and it's a cleaner dish! I also use capers, because my wife goes nuts for them. If you really don't want to eat veal or can't find it, try this with pork cutlets. I serve this with baby broccoli and pan-roasted potatoes.

2 to 4 tablespoons olive oil

4 veal or pork cutlets, pounded to a ¼-inch thickness or less

½ teaspoon salt

½ teaspoon freshly ground black pepper

1 cup dry white wine

½ cup chicken stock

1 clove garlic, chopped

3 tablespoons capers (optional)

3 tablespoons fresh lemon juice

2 tablespoons unsalted butter

1 Add the oil to a very large skillet, starting with 2 tablespoons and adding more as needed: It should cover the bottom of the pan by about $^1/_{16}$ inch. Heat the oil over medium heat until it sizzles when you toss in a droplet of water or a breadcrumb.

2 Season the veal cutlets with the salt and pepper and then fry them until they begin to brown, about a minute on each side. Set them aside on a plate or paper towels. (Note: Do not crowd the pan when frying the cutlets. If you don't have a large enough skillet to hold 4 comfortably, fry them in batches.)

3 Keeping the skillet over medium heat, add the wine and stir with a wooden spoon or spatula to scrape of any browned bits of cutlet from the bottom of the pan. Let the liquid reduce by half, then add the chicken stock, garlic, and capers (if using).

4 Cook over medium heat until the sauce thickens, about 5 minutes. Add the lemon juice, whisking as you do to keep the sauce smooth. Whisk in the butter and taste for salt and pepper.

5 Return the veal cutlets to the pan and let them just cook through in the sauce, no more than 2 minutes, and you're done. Serve hot.

> **SECRET TRICK:** If you can't find a cutlet, have your butcher cut a boneless chop in half, then pound it thin. Butchers will do the pounding for you, but two pieces of plastic wrap and the flat side of a tenderizer or rolling pin is more fun: Freddie smash!

The Icy Cold River

The journey to this recipe is as good as it tastes. It began in New York when I was with Jimmy Fallon and his awesome parents. My wife had just hosted *Saturday Night Live,* and Jimmy and I had become friends from when I had hosted the show. His father got me so drunk I apparently agreed to do a play for him in London's West End, so off I went. The first thing I do when I'm in a strange place is find a meal that makes me feel good, and I found it in the veal piccata at Cecconi's. (This place has changed owners and chefs since then, so I can no longer vouch for it, but man, back then Cecconi's was damn good.)

Later, I took a fellow actor, also in town from the states, there, too—he remains nameless in this story. He was bumming hard, being away from his family and his pooch. So I told him I would take him out to my favorite spot after the show, as Cecconi's was always open late. Great wine, great food, and getting fancy wasn't something my friend did often, so we had fun. But when we were riding in the elevator afterward, this scrawny British man who we shared it with decided he wanted to talk tough to two drunk Americans. This silly little man asks my friend if we're American. He answers, drunken but friendly, "f*ing-A, bro, all the way!" Classy? No, but he was feeling good and he was pleasant enough. The elevator dings open, and we let the Brit escort his date out first. As he's leaving, for no reason at all, he says loudly, "What ridiculous accents."

I laughed, but my friend didn't. He chased the guy outside. We're in a foreign land. It's winter. It's freezing, and I'm chasing after both of them down the Thames boardwalk! And if that story doesn't get you ready to eat veal, note that this is as close as I can get to what they made at Cecconi's, which was incredible.

BEEF BRISKET WITH WINTER VEG
SERVES 8

This is the easiest recipe I can give you for a complicated dish. First things first, this is not a Texas brisket. We're going to follow the same philosophy we use on our pulled pork and green chile stew. Not all of us have a smoker out back, even with the power of Amazon. For me, this is another walk-away dish. In fact, I'm writing this to you guys and gals whilst my yummy brisket dinner cooks for me. (Yeah, I used "whilst"—what's up?)

This is a 3-hour experience, but once your veggies are in, you walk away. Hang with the family, play some video games, call your friends and tell them to come over for the game or whatever show you dig watching. This dish feeds a small army, so don't be shy. Remember, you provide the food, they provide the drinks. That's Rule 1.

Salt and freshly ground black pepper

½ tablespoon ancho chile powder

2¾ to 3 pounds brisket, fat lightly trimmed

3 tablespoons olive oil

1 medium onion, thinly sliced

3 medium carrots, cut into thirds

3 cloves garlic, peeled but whole

1 cup full-flavored red wine, such as Cabernet Sauvignon

4 cups (32 ounces) beef stock, preferably low-sodium or homemade

3 sprigs thyme

2 medium potatoes, quartered

Whole parsley leaves, for garnish (optional)

1 In a small bowl, mix together 2 tablespoons salt, ½ tablespoon black pepper, and the chile powder. Season the brisket on all sides with the mixture.

2 In a 5-quart Dutch oven, heat the oil over medium-high heat. When the oil is hot, add the brisket. Deeply brown it on all sides—we don't need to cook it here, we just want color and to lock in our spice rub—3 to 5 minutes a side. Remove the brisket to a bowl.

recipe continues

3 Add the onion, carrots, and garlic to the pan and season with a pinch of salt and pepper. Cook, stirring, for 2 minutes, then add the wine. Stir up any browned bits from the bottom of the pot, then return the brisket to the pot.

4 Add just enough stock so that it almost but not quite covers the brisket. Add the thyme, then bring the pot to a boil. Cover and reduce the heat to a simmer. Walk away. Let this cook for 3 hours 10 minutes. (Note, you can also cook the brisket in a 300°F oven instead of on your stovetop, following these same instructions.)

5 Add the potatoes and cook another 20 minutes, or until the potatoes are fully cooked through and the meat is fork-tender.

6 Remove the brisket from the pot. Set it aside to rest for 20 minutes before cutting it, with the grain, into $1/4$- to $1/2$-inch-thick slices, depending in your taste.

7 When you're ready to serve, remove the veggies from the pot and arrange them on your plates. Add a few slices of the brisket and pour over a couple spoonfuls of the cooking juices from the pot. If you like, garnish each plate with a few whole parsley leaves. Now you're ready to eat.

SECRET TRICK: The basic brisket cut is around 3 pounds. I usually try to go for just a little less weight because I find it fits just right in my 5-quart Dutch oven with all the veggies.

THE STALKER PASTA SERVES 4

Names and places have been changed, but otherwise this story is real. I was on location in . . . we'll say Reykjavik. Most actors go out at night after work to have a cocktail, eat some good food, have some good wine. (Sometimes TOO much, but our founding fathers were guilty of that, too, just no Twitter back then.) Since my mother taught me to cook, being on location never got too lonely for me. I'd know the local grocery stores in no time, and I didn't care how small the kitchen of my apartment was, I could cook anywhere. I made Italian food a lot when I was younger because it was what I knew best: veal, pasta, pizza, and this sauce—that night I served it over linguine. On this movie, all the actors were staying in places within the same complex, so as I cooked, they could smell the garlic, the sausage, the mushroom heaven. Let's just say that for one of my colleagues on the movie, it was love at first bite. I know this sauce is good, but it must do something special to chicks when they eat it, because Sarah (also) goes nuts for it. (True.) This sauce is too dangerous to be in my hands anymore. So I now give it to you.

3 tablespoons olive oil

2 ounces pancetta or regular bacon, diced

3 cloves garlic, peeled but whole

½ pound ground pork

Salt and freshly ground black pepper

¼ cup red wine, such as Pinot Noir or Cabernet

8 ounces mushrooms (white or baby portobellos), washed, trimmed, and thinly sliced

1 box (26 ounces) strained tomatoes

1 pound fusilli, or your favorite short pasta shape

½ cup chopped parsley leaves

½ cup freshly grated Parmesan cheese

1 In a medium soup pot, heat 2 tablespoons of the oil over medium-low heat. Add the pancetta and cook it just until the edges start to curl, 2 to 3 minutes.

2 Add the garlic cloves, the remaining 1 tablespoon of oil, and the ground pork, and season with a pinch each of salt and pepper. Increase the heat slightly to medium and cook the pork until it is browned on all sides, 5 to 6 minutes.

recipe continues

3 Increase the heat to high and add the wine. Cook it down by half—this happens quickly—then stir in the sliced mushrooms and then the strained tomatoes.

4 Bring the sauce to a boil, then immediately reduce the heat so that it is cooking at a low simmer. Cook (and cook) for 45 minutes, then turn off the heat.

5 While the sauce simmers, cook the pasta according to package directions.

6 Serve the pasta in individual bowls topped with plenty of sauce, garnished with a sprinkle of parsley and Parmesan cheese.

SECRET TRICK: You can buy presliced mushrooms, but I prefer to get them whole and slice them about $1/4$ inch thick. I think they look better and aren't as dominant in the sauce. And you're welcome to use whatever wine you choose, just remember, if you wouldn't drink it, don't cook with it.

FIGHT NIGHT NACHOS SERVES 8

This is Fight Food at my house. No, we don't fight. I mean when the UFC is on, I make steak nachos. The big sporting events demand nachos. And who am I to argue? In 20 minutes I can feed eight guys with this as an appetizer for my Roasted Chicken with Lemon, Lime, Orange, and Mexican Beer (page 84).

Vegetable oil

1 pound skirt steak

1 can (15.5 ounces) low-sodium black beans, drained

1 can (14.5 ounces) corn, drained

Salt and freshly ground black pepper

1 bag (16 ounces) tortilla chips

8 ounces shredded Monterey Jack cheese

8 ounces shredded cheddar cheese

¼ cup Red Chile Sauce (page 65)

¼ to ½ cup the Green Sauce (page 15), plus more for dipping

1 Preheat the oven to 400°F.

2 Heat a grill pan or skillet to medium-high. Cover the bottom with a thin film of oil and add your steak. To cook the steak medium-rare, sear it for about 5 minutes per side, or until a thermometer inserted into the center registers 145°F, then let it rest on a cutting board for at least 5 minutes.

3 In a medium saucepot, mix together the beans and corn with a pinch of salt and a tablespoon or two of water, and heat them over medium-low until they are warmed through. Taste for salt and black pepper.

4 When the steak has rested, thinly slice it against the grain (meaning perpendicular to the grain; this makes it more tender) into 1- to 2-inch-wide strips, then cut the strips into 1- to 2-inch pieces.

5 Add the tortilla chips to a medium baking dish. Sprinkle on half the cheeses, then the steak pieces, followed by the bean/corn mixture. Ladle on red sauce to taste, then top with the remaining cheeses.

6 Bake until the cheese begins to bubble, about 10 minutes. Remove from the oven to a trivet and spoon the ¼ cup green sauce into the middle so people can dip in. Serve with more of the green sauce, if you have it.

SECRET TRICK: I season my skirt steak with the rub from my New Mex Carne Asada Tacos with Sliced Cucumbers (page 44).

ROCKY'S SAUCE

MAKES 4 CUPS

My son eats, excuse me, demolishes *everything. If you are a living, breathing creature, he is probably wondering what you taste like. This is his favorite sauce, and we do quite a few of them in my house. He literally growls when he eats it, like a baby lion tasting its first gazelle. It's cute and horrible, all at the same time. This an easy meat sauce to make on a weeknight, and you can eat this out of the bowl as Rocky does or serve it over toasted bread or pasta—just cook a pound of your favorite pasta shape and garnish it with parsley or Parmesan cheese. You can use this sauce with anything but the Eggplant or Zucchini Parmigiana on page 131, because that really calls for a meatless sauce.*

1 tablespoon olive oil
½ pound ground veal
Salt and freshly ground black pepper

½ pound sweet Italian sausage (about 2 links), casings removed
½ cup red wine
2 cloves garlic, chopped

¼ cup minced fresh parsley
1 teaspoon dried basil
1 box (26 ounces) tomato sauce

1 In a medium soup pot, heat the oil over medium-low heat.

2 Season the veal with a pinch each of salt and pepper. Add the veal and sausage meat to the pan. Cook both until they are browned all over, about 8 minutes, occasionally breaking up the meat with a wooden spoon.

3 Increase the heat to medium and add the wine, simmering until it reduces by half.

4 Add the garlic, parsley, basil, and tomato sauce. Reduce the heat to low and cook, stirring occasionally, until the sauce begins to thicken, about 30 minutes.

5 Cover and cook for 15 minutes more—aka walk away till it's done. Taste for salt and pepper and serve hot.

RED CHILE SAUCE   MAKES 3 CUPS

I put this New Mexico–style chile sauce in omelets and my scrambled eggs. I pour it over my enchiladas before I bake them. I dab it on my steak. It is the secret to my superfast Fight Night Nachos (page 63). In other words, it is a staple flavor builder in our kitchen, and we crush it. Below is the easiest way to make the sauce I grew up loving. Most people can't find the dehydrated chiles—they are dried in big bunches called ristras—*outside the Southwest. If you got hold of the dried chiles, I would have you rehydrate them, seed 'em, and add 'em to a blender with whole garlic cloves, salt, pepper, and chicken stock. Then liquefy the mixture and simmer it for 90 minutes. When you don't have the chiles or that kind of time, this is your go-to. For this sauce I recommend getting your hands on some really good-quality red chile powder from sites like diazfarms.com or newmexicanconnection.com, as it can make a big difference in the flavor of the finished dish.*

3 cups chicken stock

2 cups cold water

4 ounces (about 1 heaping cup) New Mexico red chile powder (see "About New Mexico Chiles," page 7)

2 tablespoons olive oil

1 clove garlic, peeled but whole

½ teaspoon salt

1 In a bowl, whisk together the stock, water, and chile powder until very smooth.

2 Heat a large saucepan over medium-high heat. Add the oil and let it get very hot. Add the stock mixture and bring it to a boil, whisking to remove any remaining lumps. Add the garlic and the salt.

3 Reduce the heat and simmer for 45 minutes. Remove the garlic clove and taste for salt.

4 Use right away or store in the refrigerator for up to 1 week.

POULTRY

Chapter 3

CORNISH HENS WITH APPLE AND SAGE SERVES 4

I love making Cornish hens much more than regular chicken. They're smaller, which makes them easier and more tender, and they cook in much less TIME than chicken. My mom made this for me constantly. She would mix it up based on which vegetables were in season. Parsnips or other root vegetables are perfect with these, but I like to serve this with yellow squash and brown rice.

2 Cornish hens

½ tablespoon unsalted butter, at room temperature

Salt and freshly ground black pepper

2 shallots, sliced

6 fresh sage leaves

2 cloves garlic, peeled but whole

1 large apple, sliced

½ cup white wine

½ cup chicken stock

1 Preheat the oven to 450°F. Set a rack into a large roasting pan.

2 Separate the skin from the breast of the hens with your fingers. Rub the butter between the skin and the meat. Season the hens well all over inside and out with a pinch or two of salt and pepper. Dividing evenly, stuff the cavities of the hens with the shallots, sage, and garlic.

3 Arrange the apple slices in the pan under the rack. Place the hens in the rack, add the wine and stock, and place the pan in the oven.

4 Roast the hens for 25 minutes, then reduce the temperature to 350°F. Continue to roast, basting every 10 minutes or so, until cooked through and the internal temperature is 165°F, 30 to 35 minutes longer.

5 Take out the shallot-garlic stuffing, slice the birds, and serve with a few of the sliced apples, if you'd like.

DULÉ HILL'S JERK HENS

I've also done a jerk rub on Cornish hens and switched out wine for beer. The first time I did it that way was in the late '90s while we were making *She's All That*. Dulé Hill played my buddy in that flick, and he and I got on fantastically. Both his parents are Jamaican, and I mean from Jamaica. His mother speaks to you and you feel like you're speaking with West Indian royalty. She is amazing, and his father is smoother than Billy Dee Williams. Whether it was NBA playoff games in Madison Square Garden or tap dancing and trading eights on an old-school dance studio floor, Dulé and I always had fun together. In the volleyball scene at the beach in that movie, I wrote DULE SUCKS with my foot in the sand. (Look hard and share a laugh with me.) Then I had to make up for the prank, so I made this for him after work one day with white rice and fried ripe plantains. The hens were spicy from the jerk rub, and the plantains mellowed them out. It wasn't Jamaican food by any stretch, but it is home-cooked and damn good. For 20 years, Dulé and I have had hundreds of meals together, and this will always be one of my favorites. Every time I cook Cornish hens, I think of good times with Dulé, and I hope you enjoy it, too.

NEW MEXICAN GREEN CHILE CHICKEN ENCHILADAS SERVES 8

This is my version of the New Mexico classic. If you can live without sour cream, don't add it. We don't in Albuquerque: It's always on the menu for tourists but is never used in the home. Here the cream of chicken soup in the dish helps keeps the heat from the chile at bay, so all you taste is the rich, buttery chile love. I made this dish for my wife's TV show—Buffy the Vampire Slayer—back in the day. While she was off filleting The Undead, I served her crew this dish and they went bananas. Almost 15 years later, teamsters, grips, and cameramen still approach me just to talk about these enchiladas. Cook them up for your family or for watching Sunday football. Add some enchiladas, chips, and cervezas, and you are good to go!

2 boneless, skinless chicken breasts

¼ cup olive oil

1½ pounds New Mexico green chiles or a substitute (see "About New Mexico Chiles," page 7), roasted (see "How to Roast Chiles," page 14), chopped

Pinch of salt

¼ teaspoon freshly ground black pepper

4 large cloves garlic, minced

2 cans (10.75 ounces each) condensed cream of chicken soup

1 cup chicken stock (optional)

2 tablespoons unsalted butter

10 medium flour tortillas (8 inch diameter) or 16 small flour tortillas (6 inch diameter)

2½ cups shredded Monterey Jack cheese

1 Preheat the oven to 400°F.

2 Bring a large pot of salted water to a low boil. Add the chicken breasts and cook for 20 minutes, then remove from the pot and let cool for 10 minutes.

3 In a medium skillet, heat the oil over low heat. Add the chopped chiles and cook just until they are fragrant. Add the salt, black pepper, and garlic. Stir well and cook over low heat until the garlic has begun to soften, 3 to 4 minutes longer. Remove the garlic/chile mixture from the pan and set aside to cool.

4 Shred the chicken breasts into a large bowl. (You should end up with about $2\frac{1}{2}$ cups shredded cooked chicken.) Using your hands, mix together the shredded chicken with the cream of chicken soup and cooled green chiles. Add the chicken stock (if using). Taste for salt and pepper. Stir together and set aside.

5 Grease a 9 × 13-inch baking dish with the butter and lay down 6 small or 4 medium tortillas slightly overlapping, so that they cover the bottom and climb the sides. Add half the chicken mixture, topped with one-third of the cheese. Cover with 6 small or 4 medium tortillas. Add the rest of the chicken mixture along with another third of the cheese. Loosely cover the top with the remaining 4 small or 2 medium tortillas and top with the remaining cheese. (If you want to take the time to roll individual enchiladas, then you're awesome. It's simpler than you think: Use medium tortillas and add 3 to 4 tablespoons of chicken filling—the cheese is added later. You want to be able to roll them up easily. All the leftover mixture goes over the top, mixed with stock, if using, and the cheese. Both ways work. Do what you like!)

6 I cover the dish with foil, remove it after 10 minutes, and continue to bake that bad boy until the cheese bubbles and it is GBD (Golden Brown Delicious), about 10 minutes more.

7 Remove from the oven and let stand 10 minutes before serving.

SECRET TRICK: If you like your enchiladas "wet" style, then add the optional chicken stock.

PAPA PRINZE
GAZPACHO SALAD

SERVES 4

I asked my mom about making gazpacho for this book. She quickly asked me if I was insane—who wants to steam tomatoes? We talked about recipes, and she gave me this idea. I tested it with the kids—Charlotte loves sour—and have made it more than a dozen times with them since. Bottom line, making real gazpacho is not easy. Not if you're short on time. I want your lives easier, and I want you to be able to have fun while you cook. These are all the same ingredients that are in gazpacho, and it has the same cold summer soup vibe with just 20 minutes of work in the kitchen. My kids help with everything from slicing (with my help), to mixing, seasoning, and arranging. This meal is fresh, light, and crazy healthy, and I add freshly sliced bread to each plate and place the entire salad on top, Papa Prinze style, which makes it filling, too.

DRESSING

6 tablespoons fresh lime juice

Pinch of salt

Pinch of freshly ground black pepper

2 to 4 tablespoons extra virgin olive oil

SALAD

1½ cups shredded cooked chicken (from about 2 breasts)

1½ cups chopped tomatoes

1 cup diced cucumber

½ cup diced bell pepper

¼ cup chopped green onion

1 avocado, cubed

2 cups chopped romaine lettuce

4 thin slices good bread, toasted

1 Make the dressing: In a small jar or bowl, whisk together the lime juice, salt, pepper, and olive oil, starting with 2 tablespoons oil and adding more to taste.

2 Prep the salad: In a large bowl, combine the chicken, tomatoes, cucumber, bell pepper, green onion, and avocado. Add half of the dressing and toss to mix. Season to taste with more salt, pepper, or lime juice.

3 In another large bowl, toss the chopped lettuce with the rest of the dressing.

4 To serve the salads, lay a piece of the toast in the center of each plate. Top with one-fourth of the dressed lettuce, then one-fourth of the chopped vegetable mixture. Enjoy immediately.

PUERTO-RICAN/NEW MEXICAN FRIED CHICKEN SERVES 4

I had really great fried chicken for the first time in Puerto Rico. My grandmother went to the backyard, chopped the head off a chicken, plucked it, prepped it, and fried it. Yeah, I freaked a little . . . then I ate it: Every bite was perfect. Crispy and juicy . . . perfect. The first time I made this version—my version—was in 1994 with my mother. I had just graduated from high school and was getting ready to move to California to take over the family business (acting). As you know, my mom had encouraged me to attend cooking school, but I told her I didn't think I had to go, because I already knew how to cook. She laughed and asked me to prove it by making her something she hadn't had before. CHALLENGE!! The result was this dish. The addition of the New Mexico red chile powder gives a wonderful color to the skin when it is fried and a warm, rich flavor—even my mother was impressed. By impressed, I mean she grinned and told me to get my ass in school. However, a grin from my mom on something you cook was no freaking joke! I don't make this often, but when I do, you better believe I go for it. I literally have to fry two whole chickens (at minimum) when I make this because Sarah tells everyone we love, "It's on!" and they come running over to our house. I serve this dish with two vegetables and you should, too: Something green, and something else, please. . . .

1½ cups all-purpose flour

2½ tablespoons New Mexico red or ancho chile powder

1 tablespoon garlic powder

2 teaspoons salt

1 teaspoon freshly ground black pepper

2 large eggs

Canola oil, for deep-frying

1 whole chicken, cut into parts and patted dry

1 Set a wire rack over a baking sheet and line a large platter or bowl with several layers of paper towels.

2 In a large bowl, stir together the flour, chile powder, garlic powder, salt, and black pepper. Taste for salt and add more if necessary—it should be slightly salty to the taste. Beat the eggs together in a medium bowl.

3 In a Dutch oven or heavy-bottomed pot, heat 3 to 4 inches of canola oil to medium-high (around 350°F), or until the oil begins to shimmer.

4 Working with 1 piece at a time, lightly cover the chicken parts with the flour mixture and set them aside on the wire rack. When all are covered, dunk the chicken parts in the beaten eggs, then return them to the bowl with the flour, using your hands to make sure the entire piece is covered with flour. Shake off the excess flour and place the pieces back on the rack.

5 Using caution, add the chicken to the oil 1 piece at a time, making sure not to overcrowd the pot. Work in batches if you need to. The chicken cooks quickly; after about 7 minutes, flip each piece and fry for 7 minutes more—monitor your heat. GBD is your rule here (Golden Brown Delicious); if the chicken starts to get too brown, reduce your heat.

6 When the chicken is done (when the juices run clear, or a thermometer inserted into the center of a chicken piece such as a thigh registers 165°F), remove the chicken from the oil to the large platter or bowl lined with paper towels and serve when all the pieces are fried.

SECRET TRICK: You are welcome to just grab your favorite parts and dress them instead of using a whole chicken.

FULL BELLY CHICKEN CLUBS

MAKES 2 SANDWICHES

I made two dozen of these sandwiches years ago when I was a Dodgers season ticket holder. As a kid, I grew up in Albuquerque and was a big Dukes fan. (They were the AAA baseball team representing the Dodgers back then.) When I started making a good living, I leased a suite at the Dodgers' stadium in Chavez Ravine to watch the games, and would loan it out to local schools so kids could see a game from high up top. Sneaking 20-plus sandwiches into a secure location is no easy feat. (Yes, you can also double, triple, or otherwise multiply this recipe to feed any number of sandwich eaters you like.) I wrapped half of them in a Dodgers picnic blanket to carry, and my wife and coconspirator helped me with the rest. (Pretty ladies get hassled less often.) Everyone there asked what kind of sandwiches I had made. I just said, "chicken clubs." That was it. I didn't want to hear about lactose-this, or any "what specific grain did the chickens eat" nonsense! Shockingly . . . I got no complaints, just empty plates and full bellies. And Nomar Garciaparra hit a three-run bomb to left center. So: a good day. P.S. You can use any bun, but I'm into pretzel bread right now. I also prefer to use lean, low-sodium bacon, which reduces the salt and fat.

4 slices bacon

2 chicken breast cutlets

¼ teaspoon salt

¼ teaspoon freshly ground black pepper

2 large buns or sandwich rolls, toasted

2 tablespoons butter, mayo, or pesto (page 157)

2 New Mexico green chiles, roasted (see "How to Roast Chiles," page 14) and roughly chopped

½ cup shredded Monterey Jack cheese

4 to 6 bread and butter pickle slices

2 slices tomato

recipe continues

1 In a medium skillet, cook the bacon over medium-low heat until it is crispy. Set it aside on a paper towel and use another to wipe the bacon grease from the pan.

2 Season the chicken cutlets with the salt and pepper and return the skillet to medium heat. Add the chicken and cook until it begins to brown on the bottom, about 3 minutes. Flip the cutlets over and cook until the chicken is cooked through, about 3 minutes more. Remove the chicken to a cutting board.

3 Spread each side of the buns with $1/2$ tablespoon of mayo, butter, or pesto. Add the chicken, then the chile and the cheese to the bottom side of the bun. Top with the pickle slices, tomato, and bacon. Carefully place the top bun on the bottom bun, slice the sandwiches in half, and serve.

SECRET TRICK: If you have a steady hand, you can make chicken cutlets yourself: Place the chicken breast on a cutting board and one hand on the chicken breast, and then use a thin, sharp knife to carefully slice horizontally through the middle. If you tenderize them—cover them with wax paper and pound them a bit with a rolling pin or meat mallet—even better.

PICKY EATERS

People in the town I live in now (Los Angeles) have a hard time making decisions. Even worse, they're incredibly picky. They won't tell you what they want, but they don't like any of the ideas you come up with. "I'm so hungry," they say.

"How about sushi?"

"No, not sushi."

"Okay, what about BBQ?"

"No, not BBQ . . . I don't quite know."

Oh, this happens in your city, too? What is that all about? How come no one can decide what or where they want to eat? My guess is no one cooks at home anymore: They're content to chomp Big Macs until they actually look like Mayor McCheese. My mother never gave me any say on what we were going to eat. She cooked. We ate. If I didn't, and this only happened once, my breakfast the next day was dinner from the night before. Yes, mothers, you may use that weapon, as my mom is now retired. The lesson to all who cook . . . don't ask, just cook. Did Nomar ask the pitcher what he was throwing? No, he just swung, and everyone ate it up. Also, if you eat this when your favorite team is playing, they will win. That is a guarantee from an actor . . . so it must be true.

LAST-MINUTE CHICKEN THIGHS WITH EASY BLACK BEANS AND RICE SERVES 4

Our first child had my wife on the ropes. Friends would ask, "When is the baby due, Sarah?" "Not soon enough!" she would say. Or I'd ask, "How you feeling, Sweets?" And the reply would be, "How am I feeling? Sweets? You better find a way to get this child out right now. . . . " So while the left half of my brain engaged the hyperdrive engine to make a fast getaway, the creative side thought of easy solutions. Spicy food and dark meat. I went to work and got some good smells going. This relaxed the Pregnant Wife. We want to keep her calm yet hopeful with those sweet smells, encouraging patience. This meal was a hit. The wife finally slept and the next day. Boom! Baby girl!!! And I lived through it.

1 cup white rice

¼ cup olive oil

8 boneless, skinless chicken thighs

1 teaspoon garlic powder

1 teaspoon salt

½ teaspoon freshly ground black pepper

2½ teaspoons ancho chile powder

4 cups (32 ounces) chicken stock

1 can (15 ounces) reduced-sodium black beans, drained

1 Cook the rice according to package directions.

2 In a Dutch oven or a large heavy-bottomed pot, heat the oil over medium heat.

3 Dust the chicken thighs with the garlic powder, salt, pepper, and 1½ teaspoons of the ancho powder. Add the chicken thighs to the hot oil and brown well on both sides, about 5 minutes per side.

4 Add the remaining 1 teaspoon ancho powder and 2 to 3 cups chicken stock to just about, but not quite, cover the chicken. Bring the liquid to a simmer and let the chicken thighs cook until the juices run clear and a thermometer inserted into the center registers 165°F, 15 to 20 minutes. Taste for salt and pepper and keep warm.

5 While the chicken cooks, in a small saucepan, combine the black beans, $1/4$ cup chicken stock, and a pinch each of salt and pepper. Bring to a quick boil, then reduce the heat to low and let the beans simmer until the chicken and rice are done.

6 To serve, put a large spoonful of the beans and the cooked rice on each plate. Add 2 of the thighs, slightly layered piece over piece. Drizzle on a little of the extra sauce left in the pot from cooking the chicken and serve immediately.

ROASTED CHICKEN WITH LEMON, LIME, ORANGE, AND MEXICAN BEER SERVES 4 TO 6

This is my standard UFC Night Dinner. UFC, or Ultimate Fighting Championship games, focus on different forms and styles of martial arts, many of which I grew up training in. UFC games are a display of mixed martial arts, essentially a debate as to whose style is superior, who trained harder, and who has more heart. I love individual sports—rather than group sports like football—because the contestants have no one to blame but themselves if they lose. That's how I was raised, and I expect the same outlook from my kids as well. I serve this with Fried Brussels Sprouts (page 185) and Roasted Carrots (page 163)—I like to use purple carrots if I can find them. Throw in some potatoes to bake while the chicken roasts, or white rice works just as well.

1 whole chicken
(5 to 6 pounds) or
use 2 smaller birds

2 teaspoons unsalted butter,
at room temperature

Salt and freshly ground
black pepper

1 shallot, peeled

3 cloves garlic, peeled
but whole

1 lime, sliced

1 tablespoon olive oil

½ teaspoon ancho chile
powder

¼ teaspoon cayenne pepper

½ large white or yellow
onion, thickly sliced

1 orange, sliced

1 lemon, sliced

3 to 4 cups chicken stock

1 can (12 ounces) Mexican
beer

1 Preheat the oven to 450°F. Place a roasting rack in a large roasting pan.

2 Gently separate the chicken skin from the breast meat and use your fingers to gently spread the butter under the skin. Sprinkle the cavity of the chicken with a few pinches of salt and pepper and stuff it with the shallot, garlic, and 2 slices of the lime.

recipe continues

3 Rub the outside of the skin with the oil and then sprinkle the skin evenly all over with 1 teaspoon salt, $\frac{1}{2}$ teaspoon black pepper, the ancho powder, and cayenne.

4 In the bottom of the roasting pan under the rack, scatter the slices of onion, orange, lemon, and remaining lime and then place the chicken on the rack. Add 3 cups of chicken stock, place the pan in the oven, and roast for 15 minutes.

5 Reduce the temperature to 350°F, add the beer to the pan, cover the chicken loosely with foil, and continue to roast for 45 minutes, basting once or twice and adding more chicken stock if the pan is dry.

6 Remove the foil and roast until the chicken is cooked through, the juices run clear, and the internal temperature is 165°F, about 2 hours total, basting once or twice and adding more chicken stock if the pan is dry. (If you're cooking 2 smaller birds, check for doneness after 1 hour 20 minutes.)

SECRET TRICK: The flavor of a whole roast chicken rests on the quality of the bird itself. If you spend a little more to get good-quality poultry—like from your farmers' market or a good butcher counter—it will pay you back big-time, flavorwise.

CHICKEN SKEWERS WITH PINEAPPLE AND GREEN CHILE GARLIC SALT SERVES 4

When I started locking in on my diet many years ago, this was a major dish for me. I was so bored with chicken breasts and frustrated with the lack of choices available. I called my mom. Asked her if she had any ideas. She had plenty. The main one being, I'm healthy enough and don't need a stupid diet. (But like Muhammad Ali, I roll with the punches, baby! Charm wins 'em over before a fight any day, and THAT is why I always win.) She eventually told me that when I was a boy I always asked for dark meat, like these chicken thighs, because it tasted better. She reminded me of about a dozen different ways to prep these, too, if you don't want to order green chile salt or green chile powder. (A yummy store-bought teriyaki glaze would be a poor man's Japanese robata, *for example, and I'm totally okay with that if you're struggling to eat right while cooking your own food.) The key to this dish is the green chile salt, but if you want, you could also use any other seasoning salt you like, like your favorite BBQ rub or Cajun spice mix.*

Salt and freshly ground black pepper

2 teaspoons garlic powder

4 teaspoons New Mexico green chile powder (see "About New Mexico Chiles," page 7)

8 boneless, skinless chicken thighs

1 cup chunks sweet yellow or red onion

1 cup cubed fresh pineapple

1 Prepare a grill to medium. In a small bowl, whisk together 1 teaspoon salt, the garlic powder, and green chile powder. Set the green chile/garlic salt aside.

2 Slide 2 skewers evenly through each thigh so you can handle them easily on the grill. (Please don't stab yourself, he says, because he knows the pain of the

recipe continues

treacherous skewer. You can also double up thighs on skewers, if you need to, just leave some space in-between.) Then make separate kebabs with the onion chunks and pineapple cubes by alternating fruit, veggie, fruit, veggie on a single skewer, leaving an inch or two on either side.

3 Season the kebabs generously with a pinch of salt and black pepper. Season the chicken with the green chile/garlic salt.

4 Grill everything for about 12 minutes, flipping the skewers with tongs halfway through, or until the juices run clear on the chicken thighs and the internal temperature is 165°F.

SECRET TRICK: You can find many kinds of seasoned green chile salts for this dish online, but it's cooler to just make your own from salt and ground dried New Mexico green chile powder available from sites like diazfarms.com or newmexicanconnection.com.

THANKSGIVING TURKEY, GRAVY, AND SAUSAGE STUFFING

SERVES 6 TO 8

I have been making Thanksgiving dinner for 20 years—from all by myself to now with my family. I really love it. Early on in Sarah's and my relationship, we were the home for outcasts. People with no family out here in California, those who didn't have the cash or time to fly home, or the recently dumped. The miserable and lonely were all invited, every year, for smiles, laughs, drinks, and a full belly. Years later, my wife did a show with the Great One! The late, great Robin Williams. Robin and I got along very well. He had never met my father, but often said getting to know me was what he hoped getting to know my father would have been like. I have a natural soft spot for comedians and respect them more than any other type of artist. (Sorry, actors, painters, sculptors: Try and make someone laugh who doesn't want to, then we can talk.) Anyway, we spoke of having a dual-family Thanksgiving. His family and now his "TV daughter" Sarah, whom he adored. As we humans often do, we spoke about this or any big dinner over and over, neither of us making the other step up and making real plans. We all go through this. We're all guilty. "Yeah, dinner next week!" "Absolutely!" But next week comes and goes.

When we lost Robin, it hit us like it hit the world. Brutal. An anvil dropped right on our chests. Only, unlike the ACME brand and Wile E. Coyote, the real stuff is harder to shake off. We never had our Thanksgiving with Robin, but I'm thankful for knowing him. I'm thankful for his honesty. And I'm thankful he told me my dad's mustache was, as he said, "the real deal." I'm sharing this with you, my fellow humans, not to preach at you but to encourage you to make the time. Grab your loved ones and make a date. Once a week, once a month, or once a year. Make those dates and get those memories. Tell them your most embarrassing story, or listen to their pain and share a laugh. That's what every meal should be about. Love y'all. Enjoy. We serve our turkey with gravy, mashed potatoes, the Easiest Stuffing on Earth (page 93), Charlie's Spaghetti Squash (page 164), and a green veggie.

4 tablespoons unsalted butter, at room temperature	2 medium onions, quartered	1 large carrot, chopped
	5 cloves garlic, peeled but whole	4 cups (32 ounces) chicken stock
1 whole turkey (10 to 12 pounds)	4 fresh sage leaves	1 cup white wine
6 fresh or dried bay leaves	3 sprigs thyme	1 tablespoon olive oil
Salt and freshly ground black pepper	1 orange, quartered	2 tablespoons all-purpose flour

1 Preheat the oven to 325°F. Set a single oven rack on the lowest rung. Set a roasting rack in a large roasting pan.

2 Rub the butter all over the skin of the turkey and between the skin and turkey breast meat. To do this, separate and loosen the skin from the meat by slowly sliding your fingers between the two at the mouth of the open cavity. Slide 3 bay leaves in-between the skin and breast along with the butter on either side.

3 Generously salt and pepper your turkey, inside and out. Stuff the cavity with half an onion, 1 clove garlic, the sage, thyme, and an orange quarter. Do not overstuff. Loose and light is the trick.

4 Add the remaining onions, garlic cloves, and orange quarters, to your roasting pan under the rack along with the carrot. Add 2 cups of the chicken stock and the wine to the pan (this is your basting liquid, and eventually your gravy).

5 Place the turkey on the rack and lightly cover the top with foil. Roast for about 20 minutes per pound, basting every 15 to 20 minutes, adding more stock or even water if the pan gets very dry. Remove the foil for the last 30 to 45 minutes. (You can also crank the heat up to 425°F right at the end for a crispier skin.) Cook until the juices run clear, the leg is loose when you wiggle it, or a thermometer inserted into the thigh registers 165°F.

recipe continues

6 When the turkey is ready, remove it to a cutting board and let it rest for at least 30 minutes before slicing and serving.

7 To make the gravy, strain the liquid from the bottom of the pan and add enough chicken stock to make 2 cups of liquid.

8 In a small saucepan, heat the olive oil over medium heat and whisk in the flour until the mixture is very smooth and just beginning to bubble. Add the drippings/stock mixture, bring to a simmer, and cook for 5 to 7 minutes, stirring it smooth the whole time. Let it reduce slightly to thicken into gravy. Transfer to a gravy boat and keep warm until it's dinnertime.

SECRET TRICK: When picking out a turkey size, you'll want about 1$\frac{1}{2}$ pounds of turkey per person.

THE EASIEST STUFFING ON EARTH **SERVES 8**

Don't bake your own bread. Fresh bread and stuffing don't mix. The bread should be stale. The easiest way, believe it or not, is ready-made stuffing. Nooooo! Freddie, why??? Relax. Here is what you do. Most call for half a stick of butter, but forget that. The chicken stock gives tons of flavor and saves you from the extra salt and fat demands of those American corporations. If you like your stuffing a little sweeter, go with the apple. If you like a more earthy balance, try the celery.

1½ tablespoons olive oil

¼ pound bulk mild pork sausage

3 tablespoons unsalted butter

2 cups chicken stock

1 bag (14 ounces) herb-seasoned stuffing

1 apple, cut into ½-inch cubes, or 1 rib celery, diced

1 Preheat the oven to 325°F.

2 In a medium skillet, heat ½ tablespoon of the oil and add the sausage. Cook until golden brown on both sides, 7 to 10 minutes, breaking it into pieces with a wooden spoon as it cooks. Set aside.

3 In a medium soup pot, heat the butter and the remaining 1 tablespoon oil. Add the stock and bring it to a boil. Remove from the heat and add the bag of stuffing, using 2 spoons to thoroughly mix the bread cubes into the stock.

4 Add the sausage, crumbling it into smaller pieces with your hands. Add the apple or celery and toss lightly to mix.

5 Spoon the stuffing into a large baking dish. Cover it with foil and bake (at same temp as your turkey!) for 20 minutes.

6 Remove the foil, gently fluff with 2 serving spoons, and serve. You're welcome, stuffing just got easier and better.

SEAFOOD

Chapter 4

LINGUINE WITH CLAMS

SERVES 2

This is one of my wife's favorite pasta dishes, a close second to the Leftover Pesto Pasta with Shrimp and Pancetta (page 155). The secret ingredient to both? Bacon! Pancetta is a spiced Italian bacon that is cured but not smoked, and little bit of it sautéed is a great flavor base for both your traditional and your not-so-traditional sauces. (Yes, you can use regular bacon if you can't find it.) This started out as our Sunday night Amazing Race *dinner, but it's good for* Sunday Night Football, *too. The kids don't dig on clams, so this is a dish we don't have to share. Served in one bowl, this can be a nice romantic dinner for you and your better half. Put some music on in the background, anything from the '80s or '90s works, but Sirius XMU (Channel 35) is my new favorite. Run DMC has its place, but not when you're trying for some romance with the wife.*

8 ounces dried linguine

2 tablespoons olive oil

3 ounces pancetta or bacon, diced (about ⅓ cup)

½ teaspoon crushed red chile flakes

¼ teaspoon freshly ground black pepper

2 cloves garlic, smashed with the side of a chef's knife

2 dozen littleneck clams, scrubbed

1 cup white wine (I prefer Chardonnay)

2 cups chicken stock

1 Bring a large pot of salted water to a boil. Add the pasta and cook until just al dente. Drain, reserving ½ cup pasta water.

2 Meanwhile, in a deep sauté pan, heat the oil (or coat with cooking spray) over medium heat. Add the pancetta and cook, stirring occasionally, until it begins to brown, 3 to 5 minutes.

3 Add the chile flakes, black pepper, and garlic and cook, stirring constantly, for 1 minute, or until the garlic becomes fragrant.

recipe continues

4 Add the clams and white wine. Increase the heat to medium-high and cook for 1 minute to reduce the wine slightly.

5 Add the chicken stock and bring the mixture to boil. Reduce the heat and simmer uncovered for 10 to 12 minutes, or until the clams open, removing each to a clean bowl as they do. Once most of the clams have opened, turn off the heat, discarding any that have not opened. Reserve the cooking liquid.

6 Remove the meat from the shells of half of the clams and dice it.

7 In the pasta pot or a medium saucepan, gently heat the cooked noodles with the diced clams and $1/2$ cup of the pasta water over low heat.

8 Add the whole, opened clams to the pasta and stir in $1/2$ cup of the clam cooking liquid or more to your taste, letting the liquid thicken slightly as the pasta soaks up the liquid.

9 Turn off the heat and, using a slotted spoon, scoop up the pancetta (and any clams who may have escaped) from the bottom of the sauté pan and add them to the pasta, tossing to mix. Taste for salt and black pepper.

10 Serve in a large serving bowl with a small bowl to the side for discarding the shells.

SECRET TRICK: The white wine you choose to use is entirely up to you, but make it something you like so you can drink the rest. I've used everything from Chardonnay to Pinot Grigio, but Sarah and I settled on Chard as our favorite.

THE GOLD COAST

Oddly enough, my New York clams were perfected in Australia. Sarah and I were shooting the talking doggie movie, and seafood was everywhere. We filmed in an area called the Gold Coast. Not Sydney (an awesome city!), but you're by the beautiful beach. The producers got out there first and rented these SICK houses for themselves, right on the water. I mean, I had never seen palaces like this, and I've seen a few.

Then the cast arrives, and they take us all to this tiny apartment complex full of one-bedrooms, and all of us are thinking . . . wow, I always thought you got a cool pad when you did these hundred-million-dollar movies? But we were all used to shacking up in Best Westerns for most of our careers, so it was cool. Then my friend, a producer on the film who didn't get along with the others on the set because he's actually a decent human being, shows up. This guy comes to say hi, takes one look at our dormitory, and tells us, "Let me show you where the actors' housing budget went." We saw the houses where the producers were staying. Whoa: Upgrades aplenty for us. And the place Sarah and I got to stay in was definitely NOT the dorms. It was the inventor of Nintendo's vacation house! What!?! I know, I love Nintendo!

Oh wait, you were probably wondering about our house. It was on a canal. Glass floor to ceiling, and sliding doors. A private dock we used for waterskiing and fishing. It also turns out the guy behind the voice of your favorite cartoon doggie was also a stunt boat driver, and we would go out with him every week. This guy knew everyone in the area, and he even hooked me up with a clam monger, who had a beard to his belly button. . . . I know this because he never wore a shirt, and he also always reminded me that his beard touched his belly button (Australian pride at its oddest).

SARAH'S CLAMS OREGANATA SERVES 4

Sarah is from Manhattan, but we live in Los Angeles. It's tough finding Sarah some "old-school" New York goodies, but I do my best. I wrote this recipe down on a note card when I finally got it right. These are crazy good, and I suggest you make it way more often than I do. They give you just a touch of crunch on top, and great rich flavor inside. Sarah goes wild for these. I keep the wife well fed, and if I find something she loves, it's on like Donkey Kong. (Do people even remember what that is?)

1 dozen littleneck clams, scrubbed

2 cloves garlic, minced

3 tablespoons chopped fresh oregano leaves

2 tablespoons chopped flat-leaf parsley leaves

Pinch of salt

Pinch of cayenne pepper

Pinch of crushed red chile flakes

3 tablespoons olive oil

1 cup chicken stock

1 cup unseasoned dried breadcrumbs

1 Preheat the oven to 450°F.

2 Place the clams on a small baking pan and bake 'em until the shells just begin to open, about 2 minutes. Then turn the oven setting to broil.

3 Open the clams all the way with a butter knife and detach the clam from the bottom shell. Detach and discard the top shell. Set the clam meat, in the bottom shells, aside, still in the baking pan.

4 In a medium bowl, combine the garlic, oregano, parsley, salt, cayenne, and chile flakes. Add the oil and ½ cup of the chicken stock. Add the breadcrumbs and mix everything together well.

recipe continues

5 Take a heaping teaspoon of the breadcrumb mixture and pack it tightly around each clam in the bottom shell. (The breadcrumb mixture is acting as the new top shell, essentially, so the tighter the package of breadcrumbs, the more perfect and moist the clam will be.)

6 When all the clams are packed with breadcrumbs, pour the remaining chicken stock around the baking pan. Broil until GBD (Golden Brown Delicious), 5 to 6 minutes. Serve hot.

> **SECRET TRICK:** Be sure to move an oven rack to the top level, if your broiler is on the top of your oven, *before* the oven gets hot. This is one thing people always forget to do.

SALMON AND RED POTATO SALAD WITH CHILLED VEGETABLES

SERVES 4

I really try to focus on eating healthy and putting good things in my body. This dish may feel like a lot of work, but think of it more as a template for what to do with leftover cooked veggies like the roasted potatoes and cauliflower here, or maybe green beans and zucchini. Almost any of the Four Simple Vegetable Sides (pages 163 to 167) would be great in this salad; and if they're leftovers, you know you like them. You already ate them. Take them out of the fridge, add a squeeze of lemon juice to freshen them up, then add 'em to a simple salad like this. Quick, easy, healthy.

6 to 7 tablespoons extra virgin olive oil

1 tablespoon balsamic vinegar

Salt and freshly ground black pepper

1 pound small red potatoes

1 cup small cauliflower florets

2 skin-on salmon fillets (6 ounces each)

8 cups mixed lettuce or leafy greens, washed and dried

1 pint (10 to 12 ounces) large cherry tomatoes, halved

2 small Persian (mini) cucumbers, thinly sliced

1 Preheat the oven to 400°F.

2 In a small bowl or jar with a lid, combine 3 tablespoons of the oil, the balsamic vinegar, and a pinch each of salt and pepper and whisk or shake to combine. Taste for salt, pepper, and vinegar, adding more to taste. Set the dressing aside.

3 In a small baking dish, toss the potatoes with 1 to 2 tablespoons of the oil to coat. Sprinkle them with a pinch of salt and pepper, cover the dish with foil, and roast until they are easily pierced with a knife, 45 to 50 minutes. Remove the potatoes and let cool completely, or make them a day or two in advance and refrigerate them until you make the salad.

recipe continues

4 While the potatoes roast, in a medium skillet, heat 1 tablespoon of the oil over medium heat. Add the cauliflower with a pinch of salt and pepper and cook, stirring often, until just cooked through, about 7 minutes. Let cool completely, or make it a day or two in advance and refrigerate it until you make the salad.

5 In a medium skillet, heat 1 tablespoon of the oil over medium heat. Season the salmon with a pinch each of salt and pepper. Add the salmon, skin side down, and cook until the skin begins to crisp and brown and pulls away easily from the pan. Flip and cook a few minutes more until the salmon easily flakes with a fork. Set the fillets on a cutting board and use a fork to remove the skin and break the fillets into large flakes. Set aside.

6 In a large salad bowl, combine the greens and tomatoes and a tablespoon or two of the dressing. Toss gently, then add the cauliflower, potatoes, and cucumbers. Taste for salt and pepper, and add more dressing as necessary, tossing again to mix.

7 Add the flaked salmon: One final, gentle toss to mix it in, then you're ready to serve in individual bowls.

SEA BASS WITH SUGAR AND LIME SERVES 2

The first dish I ever cooked on TV was a sea bass with sugar and lime with Rosie O'Donnell, of all people. I think I was supposed to be selling daytime America a Miramax rom-com, but I liked food more and Rosie enjoyed giving a middle finger to authority, so it worked out great. Now the original version of that dish was born out of necessity in New Mexico. We had delicious sea bass, frozen, but in the '80s for Albuquerque to even see sea bass was a rarity. And when we had the fish, we had no fresh limes. So we used frozen limeade, we really did. Now I would NEVER do that today, but that was the spark that fueled the flame that put me on TV with a funny chick. I serve these fillets over white rice with charred pineapple and Roasted Carrots (page 163) or with what I call "Vegetable Ceviche": fresh vegetables sliced and marinated for about 15 minutes in more lime juice.

¼ teaspoon sugar

¼ cup fresh lime juice (2 to 3 limes)

Salt and freshly ground black pepper

2 tablespoons loosely packed cilantro leaves, roughly chopped

3 tablespoons olive oil

2 pounds skin-on sea bass fillets

½ teaspoon garlic powder

1 In a small bowl, whisk the sugar into the lime juice with a pinch each of salt and pepper. Add half of the cilantro leaves and stir to mix.

2 In a large skillet, heat the oil over medium to medium-high heat.

3 Pat the fish dry. Use your fingers to evenly sprinkle both sides of the fillets with ½ teaspoon salt, ½ teaspoon pepper, and the garlic powder.

4 Add the fillets skin side down to the hot pan and cook until the skin is curling, crispy, and browned and the flesh is cooked halfway through, 4 to 5 minutes for thin fillets.

5 Reduce the heat to medium-low and use a flexible spatula to flip the fillets over. Let them cook until they are cooked through and easily flake apart, another 2 to 3 minutes. Remove the fillets from the pan directly to 2 shallow bowls. (If you're making rice, serve the fish directly over the rice, if you like.)

6 Top each serving with sugar-lime mixture and a dusting of the remaining cilantro leaves and serve immediately.

SPICY FISH TACOS SERVES 4

Get some sweet and spicy in your life! These are just what you want to eat in the heat of late summer, when watermelon, cucumbers, and chiles are all in season. People might tell you cheese doesn't go with fish, and you're welcome to skip it if you like, but instead just trust me and try it. Serve with rice and beans.

2 cups diced seeded watermelon

1 cup diced seeded cucumber

2 limes

3 tablespoons olive oil

1½ pounds tilapia or any other flaky white fish fillets

½ teaspoon salt

¼ teaspoon freshly ground black pepper

1 fresh Thai or serrano chile, thinly sliced

8 small flour or corn tortillas (6 inch diameter), warmed

1 cup shredded Monterey Jack cheese

½ cup fresh cilantro leaves (optional)

1 In a medium bowl, combine the watermelon and cucumber. Squeeze in the juice from the limes, mix well, and refrigerate.

2 In a skillet, heat the oil over medium heat. Season the fish with the salt and black pepper. Add the fish to the skillet and top with a few slivers of the chile. After the bottom has cooked through, about 4 minutes, flip the fish and add a few more slivers of chile.

3 When the fish is cooked through—it should easily flake apart into pieces with a fork—remove it from the pan and place it on a cutting board. It should fall right apart.

4 Add a few pieces of the fish to a warmed tortilla. Top with a sprinkle of cheese, a spoonful or two of cold diced watermelon and cucumber, plus the remaining chopped chile and cilantro leaves (if using).

SECRET TRICK: Using a fine grater, you can also gently scrape the Thai chile until a touch of fresh chile is on each one. About two quick scrapes per fillet.

SAN JUAN–STYLE FRIED LOBSTER SERVES 4

There are times in a man's life when a grilled or broiled lobster just isn't enough deliciousness. . . . It may seem dumb, but luckily through the united brotherhood of stupidity, somebody created the art of deep-frying a lobster. The first time I had it was in Puerto Rico. Wilson, my Papo (kind of like my great-uncle), was a butcher in San Juan. He would bring my grandmother great cuts of meat and fish. In 1986 he brought over some tremendous lobster tails to my grandmother's kitchen. It looked out over the backyard and was completely screened in. He slapped the lobsters down on the table, put a huge knife through the top of the shell, and split them each in half. He always looked so strong to me: big shoulders, big arms, big ol' bald head. He sat me up on the counter and let me crack the eggs. As he prepped the lobster, he spoke to me about where it came from—this old Cuban fisherman he worked with— and about what a prick Castro was. When the lobster turned golden brown in the pot, I already knew it was gonna be awesome. My grandmother turned on lucha libre *(pro wrestling, which she believed was real till the day she died) and served up some rice, sliced up some limes, and made a small salad for us. Let me tell you something right now: Fried lobster with your family, in front of a TV blasting away with men in spandex right in your face, is a surprisingly great night! You can enjoy this either as is, or make lobster tacos with cucumber slices, lime, and cilantro.*

2 cups canola oil

1¼ cups all-purpose flour

1 tablespoon garlic powder

1 tablespoon New Mexico red chile powder

1 teaspoon salt

1 teaspoon freshly ground black pepper

4 small lobster tails, cut into bite-size pieces

4 large eggs, beaten

1 lemon, quartered

1 In a Dutch oven, heat the oil over medium-high heat to about 350°F, or until it shimmers.

2 In a large bowl, combine the flour, garlic powder, chile powder, salt, and black pepper and mix well.

3 Working one at a time, dip the pieces of lobster tail into the beaten egg, then dredge them in the flour mixture so that they're fully covered, and then place them into the hot oil. Let them fry for about 5 minutes, flipping them over halfway through. When are they done? When they're Golden Brown Delicious (GBD), that's when.

4 Instruct your guests to squeeze the lemon over their lobster and enjoy immediately.

SHRIMP SCAMPI SERVES 4

Old-fashioned garlicky shrimp goodness. 'Nuff said. I serve this dish with Charlie's Spaghetti Squash (page 164) on the side.

2 pounds medium or large shrimp, peeled and deveined

6 tablespoons olive oil

2 tablespoons white wine

Salt and freshly ground black pepper

¼ cup minced shallots

4 cloves garlic, minced

2½ tablespoons chopped fresh parsley leaves

½ teaspoon chopped fresh rosemary leaves

Grated zest of 1 lemon

3 tablespoons fresh lemon juice

½ teaspoon crushed red chile flakes

8 tablespoons (1 stick) unsalted butter, at room temperature

⅔ cup unseasoned dried breadcrumbs

1 large egg yolk

1 Preheat that awesome oven to 350°F.

2 (I hope you aren't dumb like me and forgot to ask for the peeled, deveined shrimp, but if you are . . . now is the time to get to work cleaning them.) In a large bowl, toss together the peeled shrimp, 2 tablespoons of the oil, the white wine, and a pinch each of salt and pepper. Set aside.

3 In another large bowl, use your hands to mix together the shallots, garlic, parsley, rosemary, lemon zest, lemon juice, chile flakes, ½ teaspoon salt, a pinch of black pepper, the butter, breadcrumbs, egg yolk, and 2 tablespoons of the oil.

4 Add the remaining 2 tablespoons oil to a large baking dish and lay the shrimp in an even layer on the bottom. (If some overlap slightly, don't worry.) Use a spoon to evenly spread the breadcrumb mixture over the top.

5 Bake until the shrimp are cooked through and the breadcrumbs are golden brown, about 20 minutes.

SHRIMP, SKEWERED SERVES 4

Spending Christmas in Puerto Rico with my grandmother year after year meant no snow but lots of shellfish and felicidad. *My Papo Wilson always took me with him to the fish stand. We would walk up to a small podium, where he asked for oysters and shrimp. The tiny man would walk down to the nets, grab the shellfish, and serve it to us right there. Shuck, peel, shuck, peel. My job was to eat the oysters and carry home the* camarones. *When we'd get home, he would bathe the shrimp in lime juice and garlic and sear them quickly in a pan. He'd pour them over hot rice and we would eat, eat, eat. My love of shrimp has stood strong ever since. This is inspired by those memories. Note that you don't have to eat the chiles after you grill them— they'll provide plenty of heat on the skewer. I serve this with white rice and any grilled vegetable, normally the Foiled Asparagus (page 166).*

MARINADE

¾ cup olive oil

2 cloves garlic, minced or pressed

¼ teaspoon salt

¼ teaspoon freshly ground black pepper

2 teaspoons grated lime zest (from about 2 limes)

1 pound (about 24) peeled medium shrimp, deveined

SKEWERS

8 small Thai chiles or 6 jalapeños

2 cups fresh pineapple cubes

2 tablespoons fresh lime juice (about 2 limes)

½ cup slivered fresh cilantro, Thai basil, or mint leaves, for garnish (optional)

1 Prepare a grill to medium or preheat the oven to 425°F.

2 In a zip-seal bag, combine the oil, garlic, salt, black pepper, lime zest, and shrimp. Let the shrimp marinate for 15 minutes.

3 Wearing plastic gloves, cut the Thai chiles into thirds, or if you use jalapeños, which are much easier to get a hold of than Thai chiles, cut them into fourths. (Sometimes coring the jalapeños makes them easier to get on the skewer.) Thread 8 skewers with shrimp, pineapple, and chiles, repeating the process twice more so that you have 3 layers per skewer. (It's okay for the items on the skewer to touch, but let's not squish them together.)

4 Grill the skewers until the shrimp are pink on all sides, firm to the touch, and the tails have completely curled, 3 to 4 minutes per side. (If you are cooking them in the oven, place them on a rimmed baking sheet and cook them for 8 to 10 minutes, turning them once halfway through.) Remember that shrimp cook quickly: Watch them carefully.

5 To serve, slide the shrimp, pineapple, and chiles off the skewer and sprinkle on the lime juice. If desired, garnish with slivered herbs.

JALAPEÑO SALMON BURGERS WITH SPROUTS AND CUKES SERVES 4

If you're doing the low-carb thing, skip the pita—the lettuce wrap is for you. You'll need 8 leaves of lettuce instead of 4. Add the salmon burger to a large leaf, top with cucumber slices and sprouts, another lettuce leaf, and enjoy. If you're going pita, just throw it all in there and enjoy. I like mine with hot sauce (Tabasco is my choice), but the jalapeño should make it spicy enough for the rest of you. Ripe tomato or fresh herbs would also be great additions.

1 pound freshly ground salmon

1 jalapeño, seeded and diced (wear plastic gloves when handling)

3 tablespoons fresh lemon juice

1 large egg

1 tablespoon olive oil

½ teaspoon garlic powder

¼ teaspoon salt

¼ teaspoon freshly ground black pepper

Coconut oil cooking spray (see "About Coconut Oil," page 119) or 1 tablespoon olive oil

4 small pita breads, warmed

4 tablespoons plain yogurt (optional)

4 large lettuce leaves

1 medium cucumber, thinly sliced

1 heaping cup sprouts (alfalfa, radish, sunflower, etc.)

Hot sauce (optional)

1 Grease a large plate or line it with wax paper.

2 In a large bowl, combine the salmon, jalapeño, lemon juice, egg, olive oil, garlic powder, salt, and black pepper and mix well with your hands. With wet hands, loosely form the burgers into 4 patties, place them on the plate, and refrigerate for at least 15 minutes.

3 Heat a skillet large enough to comfortably hold the patties over medium heat. Spray the skillet with a nice layer of coconut oil or add the tablespoon of olive oil, and let it heat until it begins to shimmer a bit.

4 Using a spatula, add the salmon burgers to the skillet and cook them until the bottoms are just golden brown, then flip and cook until the other side browns, 5 to 6 minutes per side. When both sides are golden brown and the

recipe continues

middle of the burgers feels firm to the touch, they are done. Remove them to a cutting board and let them rest for 5 minutes.

5 Slice open the warm pitas and spread each with 1 tablespoon yogurt (if using). Stuff each pita with a lettuce leaf, one-fourth of the cucumbers, one-fourth of the sprouts, and a salmon burger. If desired, add a splash of hot sauce to each pita and enjoy.

SECRET TRICK: Salmon burgers are stickier and trickier to work with than regular burgers, but if you keep your hands wet as you form the patties, all will be well. Refrigerating the burgers after you form them also helps them firm up before you slide them into a hot skillet. Note that if your fishmonger or supermarket fish counter doesn't carry ground salmon or can't grind it to order, in a pinch you can make your own in a food processor. Cut 1 pound of skinless salmon fillet into chunks and process until the pieces are small but not yet pasty.

ABOUT COCONUT OIL

I use coconut oil or coconut oil cooking spray often and encourage you to try it instead of vegetable oils in some of the recipes in this book, like Sea Bass with Sugar and Lime (page 106). Coconut oil has some good fats and antioxidants. Better still, good-quality ones also have a sweet and nutty, slightly tropical flavor that is a nice addition to a dish like this one. If you don't like the flavor, just use olive oil instead. Natural coconut oil is cloudy and semisolid at room temperature but becomes liquid with even a small amount of heat. Just be sure to buy "virgin coconut oil" or products that say the oil is not refined by chemical means.

GRILLED SWORDFISH WITH TROPICAL FRUIT

SERVES 4

A 20-minute dish for the grill that can easily be multiplied. I serve this dish with nutty red Himalayan rice and spinach that I toss in a hot pan with a little olive oil until it wilts. If you're really careful, you can add the packets of fruit 3 minutes before you flip the fish and they'll be done at the same time.

Coconut oil cooking spray (see "About Coconut Oil," page 119)

1 large mango, sliced into wedges

1 cup fresh pineapple cubes (optional)

4 swordfish steaks, 1 inch thick (8 ounces each)

1 teaspoon salt

1 teaspoon freshly ground black pepper

¼ cup fresh mint or basil leaves (optional)

8 lime or lemon wedges, for garnish

1 Prepare a grill to medium.

2 Cover one side of a large sheet of foil with coconut oil cooking spray. Add the mango wedges and pineapple cubes (if using), fold the foil over, and seal the edges tightly. Place the packet on the grill for 10 minutes, then remove to a plate.

3 Meanwhile, season the swordfish steaks with the salt and pepper, mist them with the coconut oil cooking spray, and grill them over medium heat until the fish is just opaque, about 7 minutes per side.

4 To serve, place the swordfish on a plate, carefully unwrap the fruit, and pour the fruit and any collected juices over the fillets equally. Season all with a pinch of salt and pepper, then garnish with herbs (if using) and a squeeze of citrus.

SOUPS, STEWS & ONE-DISH MEALS

Chapter 5

FANCY GRILLED CHEESE SANDWICH MAKES 1 SANDWICH

Charlotte begs for this sandwich, but I only give it to her with something healthy like homemade soup, or when she is sick and staying home from school. Challah is great, but you can also use whatever leftover bread you have hanging around. This recipe can easily be multiplied. It's best served with Mom's "The Best" Tomato Soup (page 136).

1 tablespoon unsalted butter or cooking spray

2 slices challah bread

¼ cup grated Gruyère cheese

¼ cup grated mozzarella cheese

1 In a medium skillet with a lid, melt half the butter, if using, over medium-low heat. (If using cooking spray instead of butter, spray one side of each slice of bread before you place it in the pan.) Lay down 1 slice of the bread and sprinkle it with the cheeses.

2 Cover the pan and cook until the cheese melts, 2 to 3 minutes. Remove the lid and place the second slice of bread on top of the sandwich, add the rest of the butter to the pan, flip the sandwich over, cover, and cook another 2 to 3 minutes. (If using cooking spray, spray the slice before you flip the sandwich.)

3 Remove the sandwich to a cutting board, slice it in half, and if possible, dip in Mom's "The Best" Tomato Soup (page 136).

SWEET CORN CHOWDER WITH GREEN CHILES

SERVES 4

I make soup when it's cloudy or cold. It's just a habit. My mother did it, so I do it, and so on down the line with my kids, with luck. Those are the perfect days for stews, soups, slow-cooked meats. With soups like this one, which is made with half-and-half, you can feel a little decadent, a little extra full. Plus these flavors work great together. I just don't eat it every day. A lot of the meals I suggest are healthy, but don't think I don't eat some fried fish or chicken every once in a while. I can fry with the best of 'em; again, I just self-regulate. And by watching what I eat, my kids have no choice but to have similar habits—and so on down the line. Serve with bread or corn bread.

Olive oil or cooking spray

½ cup diced pancetta or bacon

½ cup chopped onion

4 medium white potatoes, cubed

½ cup chopped roasted New Mexico green chiles (see steps 1–4, page 14)

3 cups corn kernels (fresh, frozen, or drained canned)

2 cups chicken or vegetable stock

2 teaspoons salt

Freshly ground black pepper

2 cups half-and-half

1 Coat the bottom of a large, heavy-bottomed stockpot with a light film of oil or cooking spray and heat over medium heat. Add the pancetta and cook, stirring occasionally, until browned all over, 3 to 4 minutes.

2 Add the onion, potatoes, and green chiles. Let these cook, stirring once or twice, until the onions become soft and translucent, about 5 minutes.

3 Add the corn, stock, salt, and a pinch of pepper. Cover and let it simmer, but not boil, for 20 minutes.

4 Uncover and reduce the heat so that the liquid is no longer bubbling. Slowly stir in the half-and-half and let it cook over very low heat for 5 to 7 minutes to let the flavors meld.

SECRET TRICK: If the chiles make this soup too hot for you, try adding a drizzle of honey over the top of your bowl when you eat it.

GREEN CHILE STEW SERVES 6

When I was growing up in New Mexico, this dish was eaten in every house I ever set foot in. Every time the temperature would drop below 40 degrees, green chile stew was brewin'. Every parent and every restaurant makes it a little differently, but as long as the chile is in there, it is always delicious. My mother made this with pork. My best friend Nick uses beef. I prefer veal. What's in your fridge? If you prefer chicken, just switch to a chicken stock. It'll be amazing. The heat from the chile makes everything better. I serve this with warm tortillas . . . and the rest of the Pinot Noir I usually use to make this dish.

1½ pounds beef or veal, cut into 2-inch cubes

¼ teaspoon salt

Freshly ground black pepper

2 tablespoons olive oil

¼ cup good-quality red wine

1½ cups cubed carrots

1½ cups large chunks of celery

1 medium yellow onion, quartered and cut into ¼-inch-thick slices

4 cloves garlic, roughly chopped

2 New Mexico green chiles or a substitute (see "About New Mexico Chiles," page 7), cut into ½-inch-wide slices

6 cups (48 ounces) beef stock, preferably low-sodium

2 bay leaves

2 Yukon Gold potatoes, cubed

1 Sprinkle the cubes of beef or veal evenly with the salt and pepper to taste.

2 In a Dutch oven, heat 1 tablespoon of the oil over medium-high heat. Sear the cubes of meat on all sides, working in batches so you don't crowd the pan. When they are browned but not cooked all the way through, remove them to a bowl and set aside.

3 Add the red wine to the pan and simmer until it has reduced by half.

recipe continues

4 Reduce the heat to medium and add the remaining 1 tablespoon olive oil. Add the carrots, celery, and onion and cook until the onions begin to soften— you don't want them to brown—3 to 5 minutes. Add the garlic and green chiles and cook until the chiles begin to soften, another 3 minutes.

5 Return the meat and any juices collected in the bowl to the pan. Add the beef stock and bay leaves. Bring to a boil, then immediately reduce the heat so that the liquid is at a low simmer. Let the stew cook for 1 hour 20 minutes, stirring occasionally.

6 Add the potatoes and simmer until they are cooked through, about 20 minutes.

7 Let the stew rest for 10 minutes, taste for salt and pepper, and serve.

EGGPLANT OR ZUCCHINI PARMIGIANA SERVES 4

Eggplant or zucchini is hard to get any kid to eat. The "Try It Ten Times" rule—meaning, if you keep serving it, they'll eventually like it—is always in effect in my house. Or . . . just serve this and lie. You bread it, fry it, cover it in yummy tomato sauce, and then you can call it chicken, or some vegetable they already like, or some made-up Dr. Seussian green.

1 cup all-purpose flour

3 large eggs, beaten

1 cup panko or unseasoned dried breadcrumbs

½ teaspoon salt

½ teaspoon freshly ground black pepper

1 large eggplant or 4 small zucchini (1 to 1½ pounds)

Canola oil, for frying

3 cups (24 ounces) marinara sauce

6 ounces mozzarella cheese, thinly sliced or grated

6 ounces Parmesan cheese, freshly grated

1 Line a baking sheet with wax paper. Take out 3 shallow bowls. Add the flour to the first, the beaten eggs to the second, and mix the breadcrumbs with the salt and pepper in the third.

2 Cut the eggplant crosswise into ½-inch-thick slices or halve the zucchini lengthwise. Working with 1 piece at a time, dredge the eggplant or zucchini pieces first in the flour, then dunk them in the eggs—making sure to cover both sides—then cover them in a layer of breadcrumbs. Place the battered pieces on the wax paper.

3 When all the slices are coated, preheat the oven to 350°F.

4 Line another baking sheet or a few plates with paper towels and pour about 4 inches of canola oil into a Dutch oven. Heat the oil to medium heat (about 350°F), or until a breadcrumb immediately sizzles when you toss it in.

recipe continues

5 Cook the eggplant or zucchini in batches in the hot oil until GBD (Golden Brown Delicious) on one side, about 1½ minutes. Then flip and cook another minute or two until the other side is GBD. Remove them with a slotted spoon and let them drain on paper towels.

6 When all the vegetable slices are fried, spread the marinara sauce on the bottom of a 9 x 13-inch baking pan.

7 Add the eggplant or zucchini: Layer the eggplant in stacks of 2, or lay the zucchini side by side. Top the vegetables with the mozzarella and then the Parmesan, and bake until the cheese is melted and bubbling and just beginning to brown, about 25 minutes.

8 Let the dish rest for 5 minutes before serving.

FRENCH BISTRO ONION SOUP

SERVES 6

By 15 I had a good job at a Santa Fe ski resort, working ski patrol. They didn't ask my age, and I didn't tell: $8 an hour and free skiing to a teenager? I was all in. I never saved anybody, left my walkie-talkie off most days, and would just ski and ski and ski. Unfortunately, taking a job during school hours is frowned upon in New Mexico, and after my 32nd undisclosed absence, I was in trouble. My mother made me quit my job (which paid in cash, so that was brutal) and focus on school. On my last day of "work" I went to this little French bistro, long gone now, that served fresh bread and the best French onion soup ever. In the restaurant it was me and a bunch of Sante Fe hippies and nobody was talking—because they couldn't stop slurping their soup. The food was too good. The dish is SO much simpler than people think— though it does take patience, which is what makes it taste so good—and the presentation takes care of itself. Minimal work, maximum yum. Hope you guys enjoy it, too.

4 tablespoons (½ stick) unsalted butter

1½ pounds white or yellow onions, halved and thinly sliced

½ teaspoon salt

2 cloves garlic, pressed or minced

¼ teaspoon freshly ground black pepper

3 sprigs thyme

2 bay leaves

1 cup full-bodied red wine

8 cups (64 ounces) beef stock, preferably homemade or low-sodium

12 slices (1 inch thick) baguette

2 to 3 tablespoons extra virgin olive oil

8 ounces Gruyère cheese, grated

1 Melt the butter in a large soup pot over medium-low heat.

2 Add the onions and salt and cook over medium-low heat, stirring occasionally with a wooden spoon, until they begin to soften, about 5 minutes. Add the garlic and cook for 2 more minutes, then add the black pepper, thyme, and bay leaves and cook, stirring often, until the liquid has totally cooked out of the onions and they are very, very soft, light brown, and caramelized. This takes at least 20 to 25 minutes, sometimes up to 45 minutes or more—and is the bulk of your work.

3 Meanwhile, preheat the oven to 500°F or preheat the broiler.

4 When the onions are caramelized, add the wine and bring it to a low boil. Reduce the heat slightly and cook, scraping up the bits at the bottom of the pan, until the wine reduces almost completely, about 10 minutes.

5 Discard the thyme sprigs and bay leaves. Add the beef stock and bring to a boil, then reduce the heat to a low simmer for 5 minutes, then remove from the heat. Taste for salt and black pepper.

6 To finish the soup, brush the baguette slices with the oil.

7 Place 6 ovenproof soup bowls on a baking sheet. Ladle soup into each bowl, leaving at least 1 inch of space at the top. Place 2 baguette slices on top of the soup. Dividing evenly, top the bread with the Gruyère.

8 Carefully place the baking sheet in the oven and bake/broil until the cheese is bubbling and begins to brown, 10 to 15 in the oven, just a few minutes in the broiler. Remove the baking sheet from the oven and let the soup rest for 10 minutes. (Alternatively, if you don't have ovenproof soup bowls, place the bread slices on a baking sheet, sprinkle with the cheese, and bake/broil until the cheese begins to bubble.)

9 The bowls are still very hot: Use an oven mitt to place each bowl on a serving plate and warn your guests to be careful.

MOM'S "THE BEST" TOMATO SOUP SERVES 6

You will swear this soup has cream in it. Nope. Your friends will swear, call you a liar, a vegan destroyer! You are none of these. You're just awesome. The secret is you puree the vegetables. My Charlotte always has this with a Fancy Grilled Cheese Sandwich (page 125), and you should, too.

3 tablespoons olive oil

1 medium yellow onion, diced

1 red bell pepper, diced

1 yellow bell pepper, diced

Salt and freshly ground black pepper

2 cloves garlic, minced

2 cans (28 ounces each) San Marzano diced tomatoes

¼ teaspoon fennel seeds

⅛ teaspoon cayenne pepper

4 cups (32 ounces) chicken or vegetable stock

1 In a large saucepan, heat the oil over medium heat. Add the onion, bell peppers, and a pinch of salt. Cook the vegetables until the onion begins to turn translucent, about 5 minutes. Add the garlic and cook the vegetables until they are soft, about 5 minutes longer.

2 Add the tomatoes, fennel seeds, cayenne, and a pinch each of salt and black pepper. Bring the pot to a boil, then reduce the heat and let the tomatoes simmer for 25 minutes.

3 Remove from the heat. Working with a few cups at a time, transfer the soup mixture to a blender and puree, making sure to hold down the top of the blender with a kitchen towel to protect against splatters. Return the puree to the pot.

4 Stir the chicken stock into the puree and bring it a boil, then reduce the heat and let it simmer for 20 minutes.

5 Serve piping hot with Fancy Grilled Cheese Sandwiches (page 125) on the side.

THAI CHICKEN CURRY SOUP SERVES 6

This is an easy dish and a clever way to introduce the concept of new flavors to those who might not be willing to try them. Most Americans I grew up with shuddered at the word curry. Me too. My mother thought it was ridiculous that I wouldn't even try a similar soup out in a restaurant, so she made her own version of it immediately. An introductory, taking-a-baby-step version. (My mother thinks I'm more ridiculous than my father, who was apparently pretty ridiculous.) I loved it. Granted, I was a fifth-grader in New Mexico in the 1980s, meaning not that many curry options, but this had me prepared to take the curry plunge with other dishes as I confronted them over the years. So . . . yes, Mother. You were right, again. Great job, woo-hoo, and all that. (Grumble, grumble.) Thai curry pastes vary widely in terms of intensity and spice level, which is why I suggest you start with a little and continue to whisk it in until you've reached the right amount for your audience.

3 tablespoons olive oil

1 medium yellow onion, halved and thinly sliced

1 red bell pepper, thinly sliced

4 cups (32 ounces) chicken stock

1 can (13.5 to 14 ounces) unsweetened coconut milk

2 to 4 tablespoons Thai red curry paste

1 pound boneless, skinless chicken breast, thinly sliced

2 tablespoons fresh lime juice

4 ounces pad Thai–style rice vermicelli noodles

¼ cup chopped green onion, plus more for serving

Lime wedges, for serving

1 jalapeño chile, slivered, for serving

1 In a large saucepan, heat the oil over medium-low heat. Add the onion and bell pepper and cook until they begin to soften, about 5 minutes. Do not let them brown.

2 Add the chicken stock, coconut milk, and 2 tablespoons of curry paste, stirring to mix. Taste for curry flavor—stir in more curry paste if desired.

3 Add the chicken and lime juice and stir gently, then bring to just below a boil. (Your coconut milk may separate at this point: It's okay. Once you add the noodles, it'll be fine.)

4 As soon as you see the first few bubbles, reduce the heat to a simmer, cover, and cook until the chicken is just cooked through, 5 to 10 minutes. Add the noodles and green onion and cook until the noodles are cooked through and tender, 3 to 5 minutes longer.

5 Taste for seasoning—stir in more curry paste if desired.

6 Ladle the soup into deep bowls. Serve with lime wedges, more chopped green onion, and slivers of fresh chile on the side. Fast, easy, fresh, and healthy.

SECRET TRICK: It is much easier to thinly slice chicken breast if you stick it in the freezer for 10 to 15 minutes first.

JAMBALAYA SERVES 6

Rainy days happen to everyone, whether it's actually the weather or just one of those days at work—we've all been there. Soup is a go-to dish for many on rainy days, but sometimes soup is just ... soup. At my house, we make jambalaya. A little more excitement, but just as comforting. Plus this dish is easy, which is why every kid I've made it for now has the recipe in their house, for their folks to make, too.

Salt and freshly ground black pepper

¼ teaspoon cayenne pepper

1 dozen shrimp, peeled and deveined

4 ounces boneless, skinless chicken, preferably thigh, cut into bite-size pieces

4 tablespoons olive oil

½ cup diced green bell pepper

½ cup diced white or yellow onion

½ cup diced celery (save the leaves for garnish)

2 large cloves garlic, minced

1 can (28 ounces) whole peeled tomatoes

2 large bay leaves

1 cup sliced smoked kielbasa or andouille sausage

1 teaspoon Tabasco or Louisiana-style hot sauce, plus more for serving (optional)

1 cup white rice

1 to 1½ cups chicken stock

1 In a small bowl, mix together ½ teaspoon salt, ½ teaspoon black pepper, and the cayenne.

2 In a large bowl, combine the shrimp, chicken, 2 tablespoons of the oil, and 1 teaspoon of the spice mixture and toss well.

3 In a Dutch oven, heat the remaining 2 tablespoons oil over medium to medium-high heat. Add the bell pepper, onion, celery, ¼ teaspoon salt, and ¼ teaspoon black pepper and cook, stirring occasionally, until the vegetables soften slightly, about 5 minutes.

4 Add the garlic and cook for about 1 minute, until it begins to soften. Add the tomatoes, breaking them up with your spoon into pieces, then the bay leaves. Cook for 2 to 3 more minutes, stirring once or twice, until the tomatoes are heated through.

recipe continues

5 Stir in the sausage and the rest of the spice mixture. Taste for spiciness and add the Tabasco if desired.

6 Add the rice and coat it well in the tomato/vegetable mixture. Add 1 cup of chicken stock and bring to a simmer. Add the shrimp and chicken and stir in so that they are incorporated throughout.

7 Cover and cook over a low simmer until the liquid has been totally absorbed, the chicken is cooked through, and the rice is tender, 25 to 30 minutes—adding more stock as needed, $\frac{1}{4}$ cup at a time.

8 Serve hot, garnished with celery leaves. Pass Tabasco at the table.

MUSHROOM RISOTTO MADE EASY-ISH SERVES 4

Risotto is work, but if you stay committed to the stirring process, it will be naturally creamy and perfectly done. The point is, if you do this right, it's going to be 25 minutes of watching a pot and stirring, and your efforts won't go unnoticed.

1 tablespoon olive oil

1 cup diced white onion

1 cup diced porcini mushroom caps (about 6 mushrooms)

¼ teaspoon salt

¼ teaspoon freshly ground black pepper

1 cup Arborio rice

½ cup white wine

4 to 5 cups low-sodium chicken stock, kept hot

1 tablespoon unsalted butter

1 tablespoon truffle or olive oil

¼ cup freshly grated Parmesan cheese

1 In a large, heavy-bottomed saucepan, heat the oil over medium heat. Add the onion and cook until it is soft, about 3 minutes. Add the mushrooms, salt, and pepper and stir with a spatula or wooden spoon to mix them in.

2 Add the rice and stir constantly so it doesn't stick or burn, toasting it for about 2 minutes. Add the wine and cook and stir until has been absorbed by the rice.

3 Add 1 cup of hot stock, letting it cook, stirring almost constantly, until it has been totally absorbed. Repeat this process with 2 more cups of hot stock, adding 1 cup at a time and letting it absorb completely, stirring almost constantly. This process will take about 25 minutes or maybe longer. You want to keep the heat between low and medium-low, with a few bubbles.

4 After 4 cups of stock have been added and cooked into the rice, it should be creamy and tender on the outside with a little bit of bite in the center of each grain. If the rice grains are not cooked through, add more stock, ¼ cup at a time, letting it absorb each time.

5 When the risotto is ready, remove it from the heat and add the butter, oil, and Parmesan, stirring to incorporate. Serve hot, garnished with more olive oil and cheese, if you like.

PIZZA PIE

MAKES 2 SMALL PIZZAS

This recipe is for the pies my daughter, Charlie, and I make together. We always name our specific creations when they come out of the oven, but this is our basic dough and sauce. I've made this dough for over 30 years: with my mom, friends, roommates, wife, and now kiddos. Everyone loves the crust: I make it thin, and it's best when it has just the right amount of dough to toppings, by which I mean use a light hand, as I do. My daughter can make the sauce in her sleep. Her friend's mom, when she saw her do it, flipped out. She thought Charlotte was so grown up. When I really broke it down to this mom how easy it was for her to make pizza with her kid, she just shook her head. She never really cooked, so it was just a matter of confidence. Simply doing it. Stepping out of your comfort zone. Sucking at first, then getting better. Then owning it. Now this same lady tries to make everything, win or fail! (P.S. I let my son help with the sauce once. He just isn't old enough yet, and my favorite bum-around-the-house shirt is no more.... no more.)

PIZZA DOUGH
1 teaspoon active dry yeast

1 teaspoon sugar

¾ cup hot water (110°F)

2 cups all-purpose flour, plus more for dusting

½ teaspoon salt

¼ cup olive oil, plus more for greasing

Coarse-grain cornmeal, for dusting (optional)

PIZZA SAUCE
1 can (8 ounces) tomato sauce

Pinch of garlic powder

Pinch of dried oregano

3 to 4 fresh basil leaves

Salt

CHEESE PIZZAS
½ cup Pizza Sauce (¼ cup per pizza)

½ cup grated mozzarella cheese (¼ cup per pizza)

¼ cup freshly grated Parmesan cheese (optional)

SECRET TRICK: Tools make pizza easier. I usually do the grunt work in the afternoon, while my kids nap. But I also use a food processor with a mini pizza hook, which are easy to order off Amazon these days. A pizza stone and peel are key, too. Ditto about Amazon. You can also sprinkle a touch of cornmeal or corn flour on whatever pan you plan on cooking your pies on if you like, as I do. It makes getting the pizza into the oven easier.

recipe continues

1　Make the dough: In a small bowl, stir together the yeast, sugar, and hot water and set it aside for 5 minutes.

2　In a stand mixer or food processor fitted with a dough hook, mix the flour and salt. Add the water/yeast mixture and the oil and mix on low and then medium until the dough comes together and looks and feels a bit sticky. Scrape the sides with a spatula as you mix, so all of the water is incorporated.

3　Grease a large bowl with oil and dust a work surface with flour. Place the dough on the floured work surface and knead it for about 5 minutes, or until it is smooth, feels stretchy, and the dough bounces back when you press it with a fingertip.

4　Roll the dough into a large ball and place it in the greased bowl, then cover with a damp, clean kitchen towel. Let the dough rest on the counter until it has doubled in size, about 1 hour.

5　Meanwhile, make the sauce: In a medium saucepan, combine the tomato sauce and garlic powder. Rub the dried oregano between your fingers as you sprinkle it into the saucepan, breaking down the leaves. (Now smell your fingers for fun.) Add the basil to the pot. Bring the sauce to a very low simmer and let it cook for 20 minutes.

6　When the sauce is done, remove the basil, taste for salt, adding a small pinch if necessary, and set the pot aside to cool down completely to room temperature. (Do NOT put hot pizza sauce on fresh dough. You won't be happy with the results.)

7　When your dough has risen, punch down the center (with *The Five Fingers of Death**) to release the air. Cover the bowl with a damp kitchen towel and let the dough rise again until has doubled in size, about 30 minutes.

8　While the dough is in its second rise, remove the top rack and position a rack at the bottom of the oven. Preheat to 500°F for at least 30 minutes and preferably 1 hour. If you are using a pizza stone, place it in the oven on the bottom rack now.

9　To make 2 small pizzas, cut the dough in half and roll each half into a softball-size ball. Cover one with a kitchen towel, then dust a work surface with flour and roll the other softball out into a thin round between $1/8$ and

recipe continues

*as in the 1972 martial arts movie of the same name

$^1/_6$ inch thick, making sure it will fit comfortably on your baking sheet or pizza stone. (The thinner you roll it out, the larger, but more cracker-like, your crust will be; shoot for $^1/_8$ inch thick for a stone.)

10 Sprinkle a baking sheet or a pizza peel with a light dusting of cornmeal (if using) and gently place the dough on top. Shake gently to center the dough, if you need to.

11 Dress the pie by spreading a thin layer of sauce on the dough, then sprinkling on the mozzarella cheese lightly. (Or follow one of my three suggested variations below, or use your own.)

12 Place the pan in the oven—or if you are using a pizza stone and peel, transfer the dough to the pizza stone—and bake until the cheese has melted and the crust is puffy and cooked through, 12 to 15 minutes. (If you tap the crust, it should make a hollow sound.)

13 Remove to a cutting board, sprinkle with half of the Parmesan (if using), and let rest for 5 minutes before slicing and serving. Repeat this process with the other ball of dough to make a second pizza.

SECRET TRICK: I use a rolling pin to roll out my crusts, which gives them a thin, crispy texture. If you like puffier edges, you can stretch and pat out the dough using your hands. You can also simply pat the whole dough into a greased baking dish or small baking sheet and cook one large, thicker-crusted pizza.

Three Prinze Pizza Toppings EACH MAKES 1 SMALL PIZZA

CHARLIE'S BROCCOLI PIZZA

4 to 6 tablespoons Pizza Sauce (page 145)

4 broccoli florets, sliced down the middle

¼ cup grated mixed Monterey Jack and mozzarella cheeses

Freshly grated Parmesan

TYSON'S SAUSAGE AND ONION PIZZA

¼ cup Pizza Sauce (page 145)

4 ounces sweet Italian sausage, cooked and crumbled

¼ medium yellow or Maui onion, thinly sliced

RED AND GREEN PIZZA

2 tablespoons Pizza Sauce (page 145)

2 tablespoons pesto, preferably homemade (page 157)

¼ cup grated mixed Monterey Jack, mozzarella, and fontina cheeses

TYSON'S SAUSAGE AND ONION PIE

Note: Do not leave this pizza to cool in a room your dog has access to. Our old pooch Tyson, who is now in the big doghouse in the sky, was pretty much the best dog ever. He never begged, never jumped—this guy didn't even bark. His one weakness was pizza. He would do the sneakiest crap you've ever seen. Years ago, Sarah and I were making that talking dog movie in Vancouver. We weren't going to leave the pooch a second time for 6 months. Prechildren, missing your dog is rough, ya know? So we rented a wonderful house out of the city, in the middle of the forest. The backyard was perfect for Tyson. He loved it up there.

The house also had a great kitchen, and I cooked as often as our schedule allowed. When you're working on these flicks, it's about a 16- to 17-hour day, so not a lot of time to cook. Time off was always appreciated. One night I was making pizza for four. Dough from scratch, lots of fresh veggies in Vancouver, and lots of good pork. We did Italian sausage and red onions on the whole thing, and it smelled incredible. I used a pizza stone so the pizza cooked very quickly (and you precook the sausage), and it always came out piping hot. I took the pizza out of the oven and put it onto a cutting board to let it cool. Then I went to the living room to let everyone know dinner was just about ready.

I heard it before I saw it. I knew the damage was done. "Oh no," I said. I went into the kitchen, with that look you get when you know someone you love just hosed you. There he was, 125 pounds of awesome Akita, eating literally the last piece of sausage. He ate the whole pizza in less than 10 seconds! Sarah called out from the other room, "How bad is it?" Tyson looked at me, gums flapping, lips smacking because the cheese is burning the roof of his naughty doggie mouth. "We're ordering in!" I said, "Tyson inhaled your dinner!" We had Chinese.

MACARONI AND CHEESE X 4 [!!!!] SERVES 6

So this is the dish that made me want to write this cookbook. I'm not going to talk it up. Just make it and see. My mother would shave black or white truffles in with the breadcrumb mixture, but damn, that gets expensive quick. I know you guys can make this just as good as she could. It's easy, and after your first go you can bring the kids in on it, too. We're going to make a béchamel sauce. It isn't hard at all, and with luck it will be a strong base for many sauces you make in the future. If you can melt butter and can be patient for 5 minutes, you're already through the tricky part. Roux (flour and butter) is the base of a good béchamel, and that will be what makes your mac and cheese own the other mothers' or fathers' versions in your neighborhood. Their kids will soon scoff at the dryness! They'll laugh at the lack of flavor, and you shall take your rightful place as ruler of the block.

7 tablespoons unsalted butter

4 tablespoons all-purpose flour

2 cups half-and-half

¾ teaspoon salt

¼ teaspoon freshly ground black pepper

2 tablespoons truffle oil (optional)

10 ounces freshly grated Parmesan cheese

1 pound elbow macaroni

½ teaspoon minced garlic

4 ounces grated sharp cheddar cheese

4 ounces grated Gruyère or Swiss cheese

4 ounces grated fontina cheese

¼ cup unseasoned dried breadcrumbs

1 To make the béchamel sauce, in a medium, heavy-bottomed saucepan, melt 4 tablespoons of the butter over low heat. Sprinkle in the flour 2 tablespoons at a time, stirring it into the melted butter after each addition. Stir until the butter/flour mixture is smooth.

2 Increase the heat to medium and slowly add the half-and-half ½ cup at a time, stirring constantly after each addition. Then cook, stirring constantly, until the sauce begins to thicken.

3 Remove from the heat and stir in the salt and pepper, 1 tablespoon of the truffle oil (if using), and 4 ounces of the Parmesan. Blend until the mixture is nice and smooth, about 1 minute, then cover the pan and set aside.

4 Now the easy stuff: Preheat your oven to 350°F.

5 Bring a large pot of salted water to a boil. Add the macaroni, reduce the heat to a simmer, and cook the pasta for just 5 minutes. Drain it and return it to the pot. Add the garlic, 2 tablespoons of the butter, and the remaining 1 tablespoon truffle oil (if using) and stir until the butter has melted and it coats the pasta. Set aside.

6 In a large bowl, combine the cheddar, Gruyère, fontina, and 4 ounces of the Parmesan. In a small bowl, mix together the remaining 2 ounces Parmesan with the breadcrumbs.

7 Grease a 3-quart baking dish with the remaining 1 tablespoon butter.

8 Stir the béchamel into the macaroni and gently mix everything together with care. Layer one-third of the pasta into the baking dish, then cover it with one-third of the cheese. Repeat this two more times, ending with a top layer of cheese. Sprinkle the top with the breadcrumb/Parmesan mixture.

9 Bake until the breadcrumbs turn golden brown, about 45 minutes. Remove from the oven and let cool for at least 10 minutes before serving.

LEFTOVER PESTO PASTA WITH SHRIMP AND PANCETTA SERVES 2

This pasta was made from what we had in the fridge, without yet another trip to the store. I had bought fresh shrimp for the scampi on page 113, but Sarah wasn't in the mood for garlicky, heavy goodness. And we always have pesto and a little pancetta or bacon. The result is a pretty dish that is supereasy to make with any pasta shape—I like fusilli. The flavors are great together—and it's not too heavy. No added salt in this; the pancetta or bacon takes care of that. And fellas, a light dinner with the wife ups the odds for lovin' by like 90 percent later that night. Don't argue. . . . Just trust the homie. Hope you enjoy.

½ pound pasta

¼ pound pancetta or bacon, diced

½ pound peeled, deveined shrimp

½ cup pesto, preferably homemade (recipe follows on page 157)

Freshly ground black pepper

Juice from 1 lemon or 2 tablespoons extra virgin olive oil

¼ cup freshly grated Parmesan cheese

1 Cook the pasta according to package directions. Drain, reserving 2 cups of the pasta cooking water. Set the pasta aside.

2 In a large, deep skillet, cook the pancetta or bacon over medium-low heat, stirring occasionally so that it doesn't stick to the bottom. We want it to get browned and crispy, but we don't want the fat to smoke, so think low and slow, about 15 minutes.

3 Once the pancetta or bacon is crispy, add the shrimp. Let them cook for a minute or two, turning them over once or twice. When they begin to curl and

recipe continues

are pink on both sides—and are almost, but not quite totally cooked through—add the pesto to the pan with $\frac{1}{2}$ cup of the pasta water, just enough to loosen it up. Stir to incorporate.

4 Add the drained pasta to the skillet, adding as much pasta cooking water as necessary so that the pesto coats the pasta. Toss gently—about a minute, or until the shrimp have cooked through and the pasta and pesto are thoroughly mixed.

5 Transfer immediately to a serving bowl and dress with black pepper, a squeeze of lemon juice or a drizzle of olive oil, and a sprinkle of grated Parmesan.

SECRET TRICK: Want to make this so easy it isn't even fair? Skip the shrimp and just go with the bacon—your friends will still tell you how badass you are in the kitchen.

Pesto (Mom's and Mine) MAKES 2 CUPS

We make a ton of pesto in my family. My mama did with me. I do with my kids. Remember that. Our habits become our children's, and they are ALWAYS watching . . . dammit. It's basic, simple, and a staple of my diet growing up. My mother has greener thumbs than Mother Nature, and she was big on growing our own food whenever possible. I have memories of picking basil one leaf at a time and bringing it to my mom, asking, "Is this enough?" "Grab a handful, baby," she'd reply, "fill those paws till they can't hold any more." Now my daughter grows herbs and vegetables, too, everything from basil to beets and kale to carrots. I've found that if they plant it, and water it, and watch it grow, they'll eat it, too. This pesto recipe is mine, similar to my mother's but with pecorino Romano instead of Parmesan; it's a different Italian cheese that's a little saltier and more aggressive. My mother also adds the juice of half a lemon, which you can add if you like.

2 cups loosely packed fresh
basil leaves

2 large cloves garlic

½ cup freshly grated pecorino
Romano (my way) or Parmesan
(Mom's way)

⅓ cup pine nuts

½ cup olive oil

Salt and freshly ground black
pepper

1½ tablespoons fresh lemon
juice (optional)

1 In a food processor, combine the basil, garlic, cheese, and nuts and give it 3 quick buzzes. Slowly add the oil while the motor is running.

2 Turn off the food processor and add salt and pepper to taste and lemon juice, if using.

3 Mix it together with a rubber spatula and transfer to a serving dish or refrigerate for up to 1 week.

SECRET TRICK: If you're out of pine nuts or want to avoid them, try something really weird and add a tablespoon of fresh chives along with the basil. Oddly enough, the savory chive replaces the warm, buttery flavor of pine nuts. Don't believe the homie?! Try me! Just be sure to reduce the oil: Start with ¼ cup and go from there.

VEGETABLE SIDES & SNACKS

SWEET POTATOES WITH BROWN SUGAR BUTTER SERVES 4

This is also great with a touch of fresh thyme added to the roasting pan or even sprinkled on top as they're served. You can serve them separately or mixed together with the Beets with Fresh Orange Juice (page 168), as I do.

2 pounds small purple or white sweet potatoes, halved lengthwise

1 tablespoon olive oil

1 teaspoon salt

4 tablespoons unsalted butter, melted

1½ teaspoons light brown sugar

1 Position a rack at the top of the oven and preheat the oven to 350°F.

2 Spread the sweet potato halves out evenly on a baking sheet. Drizzle on the oil and sprinkle with the salt, using tongs or your hands to make sure all the potatoes are well coated.

3 Roast until they're easily pierced with a fork, about 30 minutes, turning them over once or twice.

4 While the potatoes roast, in a large serving bowl, mix the melted butter with the brown sugar.

5 When the potatoes are done, gently toss them in the bowl with the butter mixture. They're ready: Enjoy 'em right away. Or, if you're serving them with the beets, keep them warm until the beets are ready, and then cut them into 2-inch pieces and mix the two together.

FOUR SIMPLE VEGETABLE SIDES

SERVES 4

With vegetables, I keep it simple because kids like simple, and the main course can be the star. I also believe getting fancy with side dishes is the easiest way to feed yourself poorly: You don't need pounds of butter for vegetables to taste good, and you don't have to fry everything. (Although every once in a while you gotta go big: In that case, check the Fried 'Shrooms recipe on page 183, and enjoy.) It helps to use really fresh vegetables, which taste great on their own. We grow some of our own out here as a family (the Cali weather helps), but nationwide there are lots of local farm groups who have harnessed the power of the Internet and will actually deliver their produce to your door. Our family can't live without them: Sarah found the company Summerland Farms, and we get incredible beets, kale, carrots, delicious peaches and other fruits, and lots of great herbs.

Roasted Carrots

If it's summer, cook vegetables on the grill. When it's cooler, throw them in the oven. Roasting carrots makes everything easier and also tastier, as it brings out their natural sweetness. You can apply this extremely easy method to almost anything that grows underground, and you can also do as my mom does, which is to cook root veggies together, no matter what they are: carrots with beets or small potatoes, and so on. She'll toss them all with oil, and into the oven they go. (You don't have to mix yours, but I often do. Mom would sense my betrayal from a state away and end my life. Pain knows no borders. But so as long as you aren't related, she can't scan your mind . . . yet.) If you want to cook two root vegetables instead of just carrots, just use a larger dish and a little more oil, salt, and pepper and sleep soundly knowing my mom won't kill you.

---

1 pound carrots, peeled

¼ cup extra virgin olive oil, plus more for serving

Salt and freshly ground black pepper

3 or 4 sprigs fresh herbs, such as mint, thyme, basil, rosemary, or sage (optional)

---

1 Preheat the oven to 350°F.

2 Add the whole carrots to a medium baking dish and drizzle on the oil. Season generously with a pinch or two of salt and pepper, the same way you would season a chicken breast before you sear it. Use tongs or a spatula to toss the carrots with the oil, salt, and pepper, to make sure they're well covered. Scatter the herbs (if using) on top and toss again.

3 Roast for 45 minutes, and we're done. If you used herbs, remove before serving, drizzled with a little more olive oil, if you like.

Charlie's Spaghetti Squash

This is one of the first dishes Charlotte ever made. She was 3 years old, not much she could do in the kitchen, but she loved doing this. All I did was the slice and oven parts. Everything else was her, and she was so proud of herself. Nowadays we make this with no butter at all, just oil. (Because, as my daughter will remind you, butter is bad for your heart.) As you would with regular pasta, you could top this with a sprinkle of Parmesan or even one of my two meat sauces (Rocky's Sauce, page 64, and the sauce from the Stalker Pasta, page 59).

1 medium spaghetti squash

2 tablespoons extra virgin olive oil, plus more for serving

2 pinches of salt

1 tablespoon unsalted butter, cubed

Freshly ground black pepper

Fresh herbs, such as thyme or sage (optional)

1 Preheat the oven to 350°F.

2 Working on a cutting board, use a large knife to halve the squash lengthwise and open it up. Scoop out the seeds with a large spoon and season the cavities evenly with the oil, salt, and butter. Wrap each half completely in foil, then place them cavity side up in a medium baking dish. Bake until a fork easily slides through, 40 minutes to 1 hour.

3 Remove the foil from the squash, being careful of steam, and place it in a medium serving bowl. When it is cool enough to handle but still hot, use a fork to scrape lengthwise down the squash, shredding the flesh into spaghetti-like strings. Continue scraping until you reach the shell (discard the shell).

4 Toss with a pinch of salt and pepper, a drizzle of olive oil, and a sprinkle of fresh herbs, if desired.

Foiled Asparagus

Easy, easy. Foil packets are a great way to let a vegetable steam itself while you focus on dinner. Choose the cooking method—broiler or grill—depending on how you are making the rest of your meal. You could do these in the oven, too, but it may take another 5 minutes to cook through.

½ pound asparagus, tough ends trimmed

½ tablespoon coconut or extra virgin olive oil (see "About Coconut Oil," page 119)

¼ teaspoon salt
Freshly ground black pepper

1 Prepare a grill to high or preheat the broiler.

2 In a bowl or on a rimmed baking sheet, toss the asparagus with the oil, then season with the salt and pepper.

3 Wrap the spears well in 2 layers of foil and cook on the grill or under the broiler for about 12 minutes. Remove from the heat and let sit for 5 minutes before opening carefully, watching for steam. Serve hot or at room temperature.

Truffled Corn

Don't be afraid of the freezer! Good-quality frozen veggies are blast-frozen right after they're picked and retain most of their nutrients and flavor. I add just a little truffle oil to make superior sweet corn—it adds a little something special. You can keep your truffle oil in the fridge if you don't use it often, and it'll stay flavorful for at least a year.

1 bag (10 ounces) frozen corn niblets

2 tablespoons water
½ teaspoon truffle olive oil

¼ teaspoon salt
Freshly ground black pepper

In a small saucepan, combine the corn, water, oil, and salt. Cover and cook over medium-low heat for 10 minutes. Taste for salt and add a little pepper. Done!

EASY EGGPLANT PACKETS SERVES 4

Most eggplant dishes are fried or roasted with lots of oil, which eggplants love to soak up. Poaching or steaming them might seem strange, but it's a common way to cook them in Asia and Italy, too. It's also super easy and tastes great. As you know by now, I like to use my grill when I can, so I usually just toss this packet on the grill, for about 15 minutes over medium, if I have it going, and you should, too—or you could even use your toaster oven. I sometimes add a few sliced shiitake mushrooms or use leftover sake, which is Japanese rice wine, instead of rice wine vinegar.

2 Japanese or small eggplants (about ¾ pound)

¼ cup rice wine vinegar, plus more for serving

½ cup chicken stock

1 teaspoon sesame oil (optional)

Snipped chives or toasted sesame seeds, for garnish (optional)

1 Preheat the oven to 400°F. Trim the stems from the eggplants and cut them into ½-inch cubes.

2 Place the eggplant cubes on two large (20-inch) sheets of heavy-duty foil. Gather up the edges of the foil around the eggplant until it forms a bowl. Add your liquids and carefully close the foil, pinching the edges together to form a tight seal.

3 Place the foil packet on a baking sheet and bake for 15 minutes.

4 Open the packets carefully and drain out as much of the liquid as you can into the sink. Remove the eggplant cubes to a serving bowl. Drizzle on a little extra rice wine vinegar, to taste, and the sesame oil, if using. Toss to coat, and top with chives or sesame seeds, if you like.

BEETS WITH FRESH ORANGE JUICE

SERVES 4

I get my kids to eat vegetables in a lot of different ways, and one of my go-to recipes is for humble beets. My daughter actually learned to grow beets at 3 years old in our garden—root vegetables are easier to grow than you think, and I don't know a kid who doesn't like digging in the dirt. We also grow our own oranges, as well as lemons and kumquats. Even if you're not in citrus territory, root vegetables are grown nationwide and are available throughout the winter, which makes them way cheaper than tomatoes and other vegetables in the winter for most people. They taste better in winter, too. Root veggies in particular are also money when dealing with spazoid actors who claim to have all kinds of "new and improved" food allergies to make them stand out from their peers. (Oh yes, America, actors are as insecure as you are, if not more so.) Everyone can eat a root vegetable. (Find someone with the guts to say they're allergic to carrots. I dare you!) They're also filling, and a solid substitute to those who can't enjoy meat. So pity them no more. As I like to say, beets make it all better.

2 pounds medium beets
1 tablespoon olive oil

¼ teaspoon salt

¼ cup freshly squeezed orange juice

1 Preheat the oven to 400°F.

2 Scrub the beets well and then cut them into quarters—halve any large pieces to make sure they're all about the same size.

3 Spread them out evenly on a baking sheet. Drizzle on the oil, sprinkle with the salt, and toss to coat. Roast until they're easily pierced with a knife through the center, about 35 minutes, flipping them with a spatula or a large spoon halfway through.

recipe continues

4 When the beets are done, give them a 1-minute bath in the orange juice in a serving bowl, tossing all the beets to make sure they are well dressed. (Note: If you've let the beets cool enough to peel them, you might need to let them sit a little longer in the orange juice to soak up the flavor.) Serve them right away as is, or mix them with the Sweet Potatoes with Brown Sugar Butter (page 161).

SECRET TRICK: If your beets are smooth and pretty with thin peels, just leave them unpeeled—you can even leave a little bit of the stem end. If the peels are thick, ugly, or you just don't like to eat them, let these cool slightly before you dress them in the orange juice, and use a paper towel to gently scrub off the peels.

PAN-ROASTED RED POTATOES WITH ROSEMARY SERVES 4

Low heat is the trick to crunch and color on the outside, and warm and soft potato goodness on the inside. Plus, if you're really sneaky, you don't even need a utensil to cook this dish once you cut the potatoes.

1 tablespoon olive oil

1 to 1½ pounds medium red potatoes (about 6), cut into ½-inch cubes

1 teaspoon salt

½ teaspoon freshly ground black pepper

½ teaspoon dried rosemary

2 tablespoons unsalted butter

1 Heat the oil in a medium saucepan or large sauté pan with a lid (large enough to hold the potatoes in a single layer) over medium-low heat.

2 Add the potatoes, season them with the salt and pepper, and sprinkle with the rosemary. Cover and cook for 10 minutes.

3 Add the butter, let it melt a bit, and give the potatoes a good shake with the lid on. (Or, if you're cautious about the shake, use a spatula or wooden spoon to toss the potatoes with the butter.)

4 Cook the potatoes, covered, until they're cooked through, about 10 minutes. Taste for salt and pepper and serve hot.

GRILLED NEW MEXICO CORN ON THE COB SERVES 4

Watch the grill and turn the corn often to make sure the husks don't burn too badly on either side. You'll still get a few blackened pieces, but that's okay.

4 ears of corn, still in their husks

Coconut oil cooking spray (see "About Coconut Oil," page 119)

1 teaspoon ancho chile powder

Salt and freshly ground black pepper

2 tablespoons honey

1 lime, halved

1 Prepare a grill to medium. Line a rimmed baking sheet with wax or parchment paper.

2 Pull the husks down to the stem of each ear of corn but not all the way off. Remove as much of the silk as you can. Leaving the husks pulled down, spray each ear with the coconut cooking spray and lay the ears on the baking sheet. Gently sprinkle the ears with the ancho powder and salt and black pepper to taste, making sure to get all sides. Drizzle them with the honey.

3 Wrap the husks carefully back up over the corn, being careful to cover all the kernels, or else they will burn. Grill over medium heat for 20 to 25 minutes, turning often so that the whole ear is grilled and it cooks evenly. (If you cover the grill, they will cook slightly faster.)

4 Remove the husks carefully—watching the steam—and squeeze the lime evenly over the corn. Enjoy.

ARTICHOKES OF DEATH
SERVES 2

Of course, my wife loves the ONE vegetable that stabs you repeatedly every time you cook it. . . . She's lucky I dig her so much. This results in two artichoke courses—the leaves and then the hearts (three, if you follow my secret trick).

1 large clove garlic

1 tablespoon unsalted butter, at room temperature

2 large or jumbo artichokes

¼ teaspoon salt

¼ teaspoon freshly ground black pepper

Extra virgin olive oil, for drizzling

¼ cup freshly grated Parmesan cheese

1 Preheat the oven to 425°F.

2 Mince and then crush the garlic clove with the flat side of a knife into a paste (or use a garlic press). In a small bowl, blend it together with the butter.

3 While the oven gets hot, grab your shears or scissors and give your 'choke a haircut. If you haven't trimmed an artichoke before, you will prick yourself, so grin and bear it or wear some gloves. Use the scissors or shears to cut the sharp points off the leaves. (I start trimming the bottom, and then work my way to the top in a circle.) When you're done, pull the trimmed leaves out and away from the heart.

4 Working over a large piece of heavy-duty foil, spread the garlic-butter around and between the leaves and core of the trimmed artichoke. Season it all well with the salt and pepper and drizzle oil over the top and sides. (That last step is easier if you fold the foil up around the artichoke to keep it standing upright.)

5 Once you're done, wrap it up snugly in the foil and place it in a baking dish or on a rimmed baking sheet. Roast for 1 hour 10 minutes.

recipe continues

6 Remove the artichokes from the oven and open the foil carefully—it'll release steam—using tongs or 2 forks if you're extra shy. Let the artichokes cool for 5 minutes, or until you can easily handle them. The leaves should pull right off now: Place them on a plate and sprinkle them with Parmesan.

7 While your dinner companion eats the leaves, use a teaspoon to gently remove the fuzz and tiny leaves on top of the artichoke heart, discarding or frying the leaves as per my secret trick. Quarter the artichoke heart and add it to the plate with a little more olive oil and a pinch of salt or Parmesan. Enjoy.

SECRET TRICK: You can just trash 'em, but I like to fry the baby leaves that you remove from the artichoke heart in canola oil over medium heat for 1 to 2 minutes. Serve them on whatever meat you're eating that night for a crispy, lemony treat.

PEACHES AND PROSCIUTTO SERVES 2

Simple, simple. The classic version of this snack would be to wrap salty-sweet cured slices of Italian prosciutto around a big slice of melon and cover it with freshly squeezed lemon juice, olive oil, and cracked black pepper. But we're not doing that—forget cantaloupe. It's boring, and most of the ones from the supermarket aren't sweet enough anyway. Think ripe peaches, people . . . peaches! I also lose the oil and pepper. This is a great snack for Charlie and Rocky, too, though Rocky deconstructs every meal and eats the ingredients one at a time. (Which is funny, because that's exactly what my mom always does, too.)

4 paper-thin slices prosciutto

1 lemon, halved

1 peach, quartered

1 Lay the prosciutto out on a baking sheet. Squeeze the lemon juice evenly over the slices of prosciutto.

2 Wrap a slice of ham around each peach quarter and then give it to me . . . I mean, eat them.

3 Repeat with more peaches and ham, if desired.

SOUTHERN CALIFORNIA GUACAMOLE SERVES 4

Guacamole is a staple of Southern California living. Avocados literally grow in all our backyards. (Just like all British people live in castles, right?) At my house we make this once a week nearly all year round, and both kids crush it. No, they really do: They make this with me, mashing the avocado, and have a ball doing it. My son, Rocky, squishes it between his fingers and laughs like a madman. (We don't eat the part he helps with.) Then we add this to tacos, breakfast, salads, and of course, chips! You can also use the Green Sauce (page 15) as a guacamole if you want, but remember, the consistency is going to be smoother and looser.

2 avocados

1 medium vine-ripened tomato, diced

¼ teaspoon onion powder

½ to 1 teaspoon salt

½ teaspoon freshly ground black pepper

Juice of ½ lime

Chopped fresh cilantro leaves (optional)

1 If you have a mortar and pestle, awesome. If not, just grab a medium bowl, a sharp knife, and a dinner fork.

2 With a large knife, cut the avocado lengthwise until you reach the pit. Cut around the pit and gently pull the two sides of the fruit apart. Hold the half with the pit in your hand, or place it on a cutting board, pit side up. Holding the avocado firmly in place, gently make a small chop right into the pit with the knife blade so that it sticks into the pit. Then tug or twist the pit, still stuck to the knife blade, out of the fruit. (Give the handle of the blade a whack on the edge of your trash can or the sink and the pit should just fall right off.)

3 Quarter the avocados, peel, and place in a medium bowl. Add the tomato, onion powder, salt, and pepper.

4 With the back of your fork, gently mash all the ingredients together. Gently stir in the lime juice and cilantro (if using) and taste for salt and pepper. Serve immediately.

SECRET TRICK: I use onion powder because my kids and lots of others hate raw onions, but love the flavor the onion adds. You could use diced raw onion instead if you don't mind 'em.

ONION RINGS SERVES 4

I often cut these super thin—¼ inch or smaller—to add them to a steak or salad, and use the thicker cut when I am serving them as a side dish. (But the wife likes them thin, so then again, I usually just cut 'em thin.) I also prefer these fried in olive oil—it adds a rich flavor.

1 cup all-purpose flour

1 teaspoon ancho chile powder

¼ teaspoon cayenne pepper

½ teaspoon salt

¼ teaspoon freshly ground black pepper

2 large eggs

Olive oil or canola oil, for shallow-frying

1 yellow onion, sliced into ½-inch-thick rings

2 tablespoons finely grated Parmesan cheese

1   Set a wire rack over a baking sheet. Line a large plate with paper towels.

2   In a medium bowl, combine the flour, spices, salt, and black pepper. Beat the eggs in a small bowl.

3   In a medium saucepan or deep skillet, heat about ½ inch of oil to medium-high (around 350°F), or until the oil begins to shimmer.

4   Give each batch of onion rings a bath in the eggs, then cover them well on all sides with the flour mixture, setting them down gently on the rack set into the baking sheet until all have been battered.

5   Working with just a few at a time—NOT all at once—add the onions to the oil. These will cook fast, about 3 minutes. Flip them over if necessary halfway through. When they are GBD (Golden Brown Delicious), remove the onions and place them on the paper towels. (You may need to add a little oil in later batches. If so, let it come back up to medium-high.)

6   When all the onion rings are fried, sprinkle on a little more salt and pepper and dust with the Parmesan.

FRIED 'SHROOMS SERVES 4

This is some serious shiitake mushroom right here. They are great on their own, or you can dunk them in your favorite dipping sauce. They're also awesome stuffed into sandwiches.

1¼ cups all-purpose flour

2 tablespoons ancho chile powder

1 tablespoon garlic powder

1 teaspoon cayenne pepper

1 teaspoon salt

½ teaspoon freshly ground black pepper

2 large eggs

Canola oil, for deep-frying

1 pound shiitake or portobello mushrooms, stemmed and dried

1 Set a wire rack over a baking sheet. Line a large plate with paper towels.

2 In a medium bowl, combine the flour, spices, salt, and pepper. Beat the eggs in a small bowl.

3 In a deep-sided sauté pan or Dutch oven, pour 3 to 4 inches of canola oil. Heat the oil to medium (around 350°F), or until it begins to shimmer.

4 While the oil heats, give the mushrooms a bath in the eggs, then cover them well on all sides with the flour mixture, setting them down gently on the rack set in the baking sheet until all have been battered.

5 Working in batches, fry the mushrooms carefully in the oil—being careful not to crowd the pan—and cook, flipping occasionally till GBD (Golden Brown Delicious) on both sides, about 4 minutes total. Place them on the paper towels until all the 'shrooms are fried.

6 Sprinkle with a pinch of salt and serve hot.

FRIED BRUSSELS SPROUTS SERVES 4

I always make this with my UFC Fight Night roasted chicken (page 84). My buddy who watches with me scowled when he saw Brussels sprouts for a fight night; then he tasted them. He and Sarah would have fought to the death for them had I not made two batches. (He would have lost, by the way . . . bad . . . like really bad. My wife is no joke.)

Canola oil, for deep-frying

1 dozen Brussels sprouts, washed and dried

¼ cup finely grated Parmesan cheese

1 Line a large bowl with paper towels.

2 Pour 2 to 3 inches of oil into a Dutch oven or deep skillet. Heat the oil to medium-high (around 350°F), or until it begins to shimmer.

3 While the oil heats, trim the root end of the sprouts and gently remove the leaves, paring away stem as needed. (You may not be able to remove them all from the tight inner core, so save whatever you don't use to slice into a salad or chicken soup.)

4 Being very careful of splattering—the drier your sprouts, the better—add the leaves in small bunches to the hot oil. Cook them until crispy and brown, about 1 minute or less, using a spoon or the strainer to toss the leaves in the oil so both sides fry.

5 With a strainer, remove the sprouts from the oil to the paper towel–lined bowl.

6 When all the leaves are cooked, place the fried leaves in a serving bowl, sprinkle on the Parmesan, and toss immediately with tongs or 2 spoons until it evenly covers the leaves.

CHARLIE'S DOUBLE-CHIP COOKIES

MAKES 3 DOZEN 3-INCH COOKIES

My daughter, Charlotte (she's the Charlie), loves baking, and I'd like to think it's because she loves science and chemistry like her old man, but it's more than likely the decorating with, and tasting of, chocolate and peanut butter chips. (Eating of the sweet ingredients as you bake is The Wife's contribution to the kitchen.) The addition of the oatmeal is old-school, from my mother. In the '80s this was her "secret ingredient," but with things like the Food Network . . . no more secrets, Mama, haha! You can also add chopped nuts to this if you want, though I avoid them because some kids have allergies, and I don't want to be THAT DAD!

I will end this with a PLEASE be careful with sweets and your children and your loved ones. There's so much crap that can kill us out there already, why make eating an issue, too? My grandmother was diabetic, and a huge portion of our country has all kinds of weight troubles, so enjoy a few cookies, but make sure dessert is NOT an everyday option. I'm not anti-anything when it comes to food, but just don't go all Roman on the sweets. Didn't end well for them, won't end well for you. (Trust your homie, Freddie P.) It also makes this more of a treat and a special thing, instead of a just-an-everyday-whatever thing.

2¼ cups all-purpose flour

½ cup old-fashioned rolled oats

1 teaspoon baking powder

1 teaspoon baking soda

½ teaspoon salt

2 sticks (8 ounces) unsalted butter, at room temperature

1 cup packed light brown sugar

1 cup granulated sugar

1 teaspoon pure vanilla extract

2 large eggs

1 cup (6 ounces) semisweet chocolate chips

1 cup (6 ounces) peanut butter chips

recipe continues

1 Preheat the oven to 375°F. Grease 2 large baking sheets.

2 In a medium bowl, mix together the flour, oats, baking powder, baking soda, and salt.

3 In a large bowl, beat together the butter, sugars, and vanilla until creamy. Beat in the eggs one at a time. Gradually add the flour mixture and then stir in the chips.

4 Drop by big spoonfuls—a mounded tablespoon works great and makes 3-inch cookies—onto the baking sheets about $1\frac{1}{2}$ inches apart.

5 Bake until the tops begin to brown and the cookies are cooked through, 12 to 15 minutes for cookies that are still slightly chewy. Let sit for 5 minutes, then remove the cookies with a spatula to a cooling rack.

SECRET TRICK: Split your dough in half and add chocolate chips to one half and peanut butter chips to the other.

CHOCOLATE ICE CUBES

MAKES 1 DOZEN ICE CUBES

I'm not joking: Chocolate ice cubes are awesome. As you know by now, I grew up in Albuquerque. In the summer, it was serious heat. To quote Matthew Broderick in Biloxi Blues, "It's like Africa hot." So we thought of cool ways to keep cool. My mom would take three of these cubes and toss them in a glass of water or milk, or even a bowl of vanilla ice cream. You can do anything you want with them: I put them in yogurt and chill outside with a sweet treat.

2 cups chocolate syrup

1 standard ice cube tray

1 Slowly add the syrup to the ice cube tray, being careful not to overflow the tray, or you'll be picking specks of chocolate off the freezer floor for weeks.

2 Freeze for 1 hour 30 minutes to 2 hours and serve.

SECRET TRICK: You can also wrap the ice cube tray tightly in plastic wrap and stab the middle of each cube through with a toothpick before you freeze them so that you can eat them like mini milk chocolate Popsicles. (But everyone does that, right?)

WHY WE COOK TOGETHER

When I started showing Charlie how to cook, she was not excited by it. But you have to stay patient as a parent, knowing that it really does stick; after enough time, she began to join in. Washing things or adding the seasoning came first, and now she even asks, "Daddy, can we please steam mussels and clams?" And so we do. This may sound weird, but when I was a kid, all I wanted was a dad I could split a bowl of cereal or a big-time sandwich with. I would always see fathers and sons or fathers and daughters at the old burger place by my house, or at any of the city of Albuquerque's many restaurants. As a little boy, I would see my dad's face everywhere. On the face of a waiter, on one of my schoolteachers. Apparently, his ghost haunted my hometown for quite a few years after he died as I tried to "work things out." Today I get to cook, grill, bake, fry, and most important, eat with my kids. And it feels way better than anything I could've ever imagined. Your kids will remember these days, forever. (They'll hate you during puberty, but that's kind of funny and awesome all at once.)

CHARLIE'S DESSERT

SERVES 1

My daughter came up with this all by herself. Every ingredient and measurement is hers—my only contribution is slicing what I'm told to slice, and eating it. We've made this a few different ways, but this is the best.

1 banana, sliced

¼ large mango, cubed (optional)

1 cup heavy cream

1 teaspoon sugar

1 tablespoon fresh lemon or lime juice

⅛ teaspoon ground cinnamon

1 teaspoon good-quality honey

1 Prepare your fruit and refrigerate it for 15 to 20 minutes.

2 Meanwhile, with an electric mixer or egg beater, whip the heavy cream and sugar in a bowl until soft peaks form. Set aside. (You will have enough to make a couple of desserts, or leftovers will last in the fridge for a day or two.)

3 Add the bananas and/or mango to a serving bowl with the lemon or lime juice and gently smash the fruit. Just a few smashes: You don't want it to be pureed or totally smooth. Sprinkle on the cinnamon, drizzle with the honey, and mix the fruit together once more.

4 Finish the bowl with a large dollop of whipped cream and serve. It's delicious. Enjoy.

SECRET TRICK: You can make this in the bowl you'll eat from. You can use just bananas or mangoes or mix them together. And you can, of course, use yogurt (which makes a solid breakfast!) or even premade whipped cream—I won't judge.

ACKNOWLEDGMENTS

Thank you to my agent Hannah Gordon and writer Rachel Wharton.

Thank you to the Rodale team: editor Dervla Kelly, art director Jeff Batzli, and designer Rae Ann Spitzenberger. Thank you to the photo shoot team: Ellen Silverman, Nate Hoffman, Alicia Busczak, Marian Cooper Cairns, Peter Baker, Natalie O'Brien, Ali Sherry, David DeLeon, Nora Singley, Alistair Turnbull, and Ian Baguska.

And thanks and love to my family: Sarah, Charlotte, Rocky, and Kathy.

INDEX

Underscored page references indicate sidebars. **Boldface** references indicate photographs.